THERE IS NO WALL

THERE IS NO WALL

ALLIE BAILEY

Vertebrate Publishing, Sheffield
www.adventurebooks.com

THERE IS NO WALL

Allie Bailey

First published in 2024 by Vertebrate Publishing.

VERTEBRATE PUBLISHING, Omega Court, 352 Cemetery Road, Sheffield S11 8FT, United Kingdom. *www.adventurebooks.com*

Cover photography by David Miller. *www.david-miller.uk*

This book is a work of non-fiction based on the life of Allie Bailey. The author has stated to the publishers that, except in such minor respects not affecting the substantial accuracy of the work, the contents of the book are true.

A CIP catalogue record for this book is available from the British Library.

ISBN: 978-1-83981-218-7 (Paperback)
ISBN: 978-1-83981-219-4 (Ebook)
ISBN: 978-1-83981-220-0 (Audiobook)

CONTENTS

This book contains recollections and discussion of subjects that some readers might find troubling, described using blunt and graphic language. These subjects include, but are not limited to: depression, self-harm and suicidal thoughts, abusive behaviour, alcoholism and addiction.

We don't recommend this book for younger readers or those sensitive to these subjects; page 172 contains details of organisations and resources which can provide support.

For Pickle, the light in my dark, forever my girl.
For everyone that sees no hope. It is there, I promise. Be brave, stand tall, read on.
And to Scott. I miss you. We all do.

INTRODUCTION

THE STORIES WE BELIEVE ARE THE ONES WE TELL OURSELVES THE MOST

Listen to: 'Ready to Start' – Arcade Fire

Apparently, there are a few guaranteed ways to absolutely captivate you, dear reader, and ensure that from the very first word you're locked in to this book and you never, ever want to put it down. These methods include but are not limited to: recounting a distressing scene from the beginning of my life; casually describing a situation fraught with danger; writing about a horrifying event that shattered my very existence; or pinpointing the exact moment I realised something was terribly wrong. The problem with these techniques is that this book is actually a horrible cocktail of every single one of them. All 192 pages of it are full of that shit, so I kind of feel that mentioning any of them specifically is a bit spoilerish. Spoiler: this book is a bit miserable! So, instead of wowing you with some kind of sad-bomb, I'll start with a little introduction.

Hello, I'm Allie. I'm a forty-two-year-old recovering alcoholic depressive who likes running very long races in very hilly places and who talks to her dog like she's actually a child. I used to work in the music industry, but now I teach people how to run really, really far, how not to be a dick to themselves and how to change their way of thinking from car-crashy self-loathing to way more helpful self-lovin'; some people call me a coach. I am now also an author, and that is fucking cool.

I don't have any huge achievements to describe here. I'm not 'special' in that way. The one and only world record I had a hand in isn't that cool, I don't have any solo fastest known times and my world-first list isn't one that most other runners or adventurers would trade off. To all intents and purposes, I'm actually very, very ordinary, and I think it's important we start there – because what happened to me can happen to anyone. Addiction and Fucking Depression™ don't discriminate. People discriminate, people assume and people say, 'It'll never happen to me'. But it can, and it does, and maybe it is right now. Maybe that's why you're reading this book. Maybe it's because you're worried about someone you love. Maybe it's because you have a feeling something isn't right and you're looking for an answer. Whatever the reason, thank you. I hope you find some of my words beneficial.

While I was writing this book, people would obviously ask me what it was about. 'Well,' I'd say, 'it's about a depressed alcoholic who realises her dream job is killing her, gets super into running and then stumbles through life a miserable fucking wreck doing ridiculous things, running ridiculous races until her whole life falls apart and then … ' And then ... my commissioning editor would sweep in – either in real life or on social media – and say something like, 'but it's full of hope, honesty and remarkable achievements; it's really helpful! Honestly it is! It's inspiring! It's insightful', and I would just sort of walk off because I don't like it when people are nice about me. I find it incredibly hard to describe what this book is about without sounding like a knob. I'll give it a go anyway.

I wrote this book to help people. I wrote it so people could feel seen, heard and understood; so they could feel comfort rather than judgement; and hopefully so they could work out what to do next if any of it felt relatable. I'm hoping that you, lovely reader, will be able to relate to it in some way, whether you run or not. Maybe cycling is your thing, maybe you're a triathlete (deepest sympathies), or maybe you don't do anything silly like that at all. Hopefully you can get something out of it whether you relate to the sporty bits or not. Just replace the word 'running' with 'fly fishing' or 'figure skating' or 'origami competitions' in your head. Hopefully it works.

I wrote this book so that people could understand what it is like to be depressed, to be an addict and to still lead what appears to be a pretty awesome life. I wrote it so people could understand that addicts are everywhere, apparently functioning like normal people. So are the depressed. They walk among us like there is nothing wrong, and then one day they are gone, and you ask yourself what you could have done. This book might help with that. I also wrote it so people could see that there is hope and there is the chance to recover, because at my worst times, for many years, I had no hope at all. I just thought that this was the way it was; that I was broken and would never be fixed.

For most addicts, addiction isn't the tabloidy social media folk devil that society likes to push at us. It's not being slumped in a gutter, shitting yourself in the street or losing your house, job or family. I'm sure that does happen, but it didn't quite happen to me.

And ultrarunning isn't the shiny UTMB-esque social media sport that society would have us believe it is either – although I have defo been found slumped against a few walls and shat myself as a result of running ultras. That has absolutely happened.

And the two of them together? Substance addiction and ultrarunning? NOPE. They can't *possibly* exist together. How can an alcoholic run hundreds and hundreds of miles and keep doing it for years? It's just not a thing. It's just not possible. But it is a thing, and it is possible. I am an ultrarunner, and for a very long time I did that as a functioning alcoholic. Running didn't stop me drinking. Sometimes it actually encouraged and enabled my drinking. I still suffer from sporadic and sometimes crippling episodes of depression. Running hasn't stopped that either.

I love running, I love the sport, and I love that I am still here and still able to do the things I do. But let me make this clear from the very start: it wasn't running that saved me from addiction or depression. And it won't save you, either.

For a long time, I used running alongside booze as both a balancer and a facilitator. I also used running as a measure of my self-worth and to prove to myself and others that I was 'not ill'. I'd go as far as to say that not only did it not save me, at times it also went some of the way towards damaging me further, in the short term at least.

At times, running has crushed me, broken me and made me feel like utter shit. It has shattered my heart and left me bereft. It has frightened me, flogged me and fucked me up. It has promised the world and delivered nothing, and it has made me feel like I am just not good enough. But it has also given me a lot. It has held a big old mirror up to me and forced me to look at exactly what was going on, even when I didn't want to see it or acknowledge it; even when I ignored it. It has shown me acceptance, community, even love, and it has bought me the time and the insights I needed to sort my shit out on more than one occasion. Running, but more specifically ultrarunning, is both the most brutal and the most beautiful way to test the stuff therapists talk about in their little rooms. It not only allowed me the space to test myself when I started to get well again, but it also gave me the time to do that. Ultrarunning was the awakening, the reckoning and the realising that led to me being able to sit here and write this today.

I am the subject of this book, which makes me feel like a semi-psychotic narcissist, but I am all I know so you'll have to deal with it. While the book is about my experience, it may also be a book about you, or who you once were, or who you want to be. It may be about your friend or brother or sister. It's a book about the confusion and fire that has raged in my head for as long as I can remember, and about the hope, patience and fight it took to get out the other side, not once but loads and loads of times. It's about parts of my life that, pieced together, make me who I am now. It's about getting to a place that I never thought possible while fighting a fight only visible to me – a fight against a constant opponent, unseen by others and only partially understood by me.

This book is about awakenings: those little thoughts that pop up, wave a flag and tell you maybe things aren't quite right. It's about reckonings: those times you've come face to face with yourself but still refuse to accept that something has to change. And it's about realisings: that expecting change without changing anything makes you fucking insane. It's about what happens when your world falls apart around you. It's about what really happens when you try to pick yourself up.

I talk a lot in this book about *not* knowing who I am. But even through the darkest bits, at the very core of me is a part that, although damaged, is the same as it has always been. I don't really know what to call it. It sits near my heart, underneath layers of dirt, dented, damaged, but still fully functioning. I picture it like a small, shiny box with rounded edges. It glows, it's warm, it exudes kindness. It wants to be helpful; it's annoyingly people-pleasy. It's a part of me that I feel I have unconsciously, maybe even accidentally, tried to destroy on several occasions, but it is there, and it always will be. I see it in me, I see it in the people I love, and I see it every time I look at Pickle. Pickle is my dog. She is also the love of my life; my first, my last, my everything. I fucking love that dog.

When Pickle was rescued from the side of a road in Bulgaria, she was so still that they took a body bag over to collect her. When they went to pick her up, they found that her little heart was beating very slowly. The box in her chest was shining. They took her in, and they nursed her back to health. They rescued her so that she could then rescue me. There have been many, many times where I totally identify with Pickle in that moment. Small, broken, unbelieving; but resilient, brave and hopeful. Pickle and I have the same shiny box. She was sent to help me. I just want to help other people.

I've spent almost three years putting the pieces together and then rearranging them to make this book make sense and not end my career before it's even started. I want it to be helpful, hopeful, but above all honest. And I really, really hope there are some funny bits.

In that time, I have had to factory-reset a few times. At times I wasn't well enough to write this book. At times what you will read is painful and dark. It was painful and dark to remember and it was dark and painful to write.

I'm relying on my own accounts written and kept on my computer or concealed in the far reaches of the internet. I'm relying on notes in journals dotted around my house and on my phone, and from a memory fogged not only by depression and alcohol but by lost sleep, stress, trauma and a part of my brain and heart that still needs to protect both myself and the people I love. Sobriety has made me sharp. The flashbacks have been incredibly helpful and at times mortally wounding. I may not remember everything, but there's much I will not forget.

The book is split into three parts made up of chapters and blog excerpts, some of which have previously been published in full and unedited on my own website (*alliebailey.co.uk*), but most are on the internet where nobody can find them. Hidden. I did this because these pieces were just too painful for me to want my family or friends to read at the time, but I needed to release them somewhere because I had nobody else to confide in. I was scared I would be sectioned. I was scared I was a burden, but I needed to put that Allie somewhere. I had no idea that some of those blogs could possibly be of help to other people. Including them here gives those terrible parts of my life some meaning, and I really hope they *are* helpful. That being said, I write openly and frequently about topics and feelings that some people may find triggering. Please look after yourself as you read through it. At the end of the book there is a list of places that can help you if you feel you need someone to talk to – about your feelings, not about how shit this book is. There isn't a helpline for that. Yet.

Music has been and will always be a hugely important part of my life, so there is a playlist that accompanies this opus; you can find it on Spotify (*bit.ly/ab_runs*). These are the songs I clung to in the darkest times and shouted from the rooftops in the brightest. These songs give me solace and connection as well as freedom and fuck-you energy. They are songs that take me back to exact moments in my life, both euphoric and desolate. They are my turn-shit-around songs, my something-is-wrong songs, my you-have-broken-my-fucking-heart songs, my nobody-understands-me songs. I encourage every single person that reads this book to listen to that playlist and chase up the artists in question. In some cases, these bands are as much responsible for giving me acceptance of myself and my situation as running and sobriety have been. Special mention to Frightened Rabbit, The National, Bon Iver, Biffy Clyro and Arcade Fire. On some occasions, they have stopped me from doing some pretty stupid shit, only because for the moments that I wrapped myself up in their words and music, I felt like somebody else understood me.

The title of this book comes from a question I was asked on stage at the National Running Show in 2019. I think a lot about the girl who asked this question. I wonder where she is in her journey now.

I was on a panel, hungover, anxious, depressed and ironically talking about how running can help your mental health. I was being very grown up and inspiring – the way functioning alcoholics can be. We are everywhere. You just don't see us.

At the end of the session, a member of the audience put up her hand to ask a question. I'll never forget this girl. She was small, *tiny* small, like a little bird, and looked extremely nervous. She was the personification of how I felt inside most of the time. She had over-sized glasses on and spoke so quietly I could hardly hear her.

She was running her first half-marathon later that year and was exceptionally nervous about it. She asked me what would happen when she hit 'The Wall'. The Wall, for all you non-running people out there, is generally described as a 'condition of sudden fatigue and loss of energy which is caused by the depletion of glycogen stores in the liver and muscles' (cheers, Wikipedia ...). It happens suddenly and can feel like, erm ... hitting a brick wall. It comes from running too quickly, for too long, with not enough fuel in the tank; it's totally avoidable. But the industry has taken The Wall and used it as a bogey monster-esque marketing hook in order to make you buy things you don't need. They have hyped The Wall into this ethereal, looming, unavoidable spectre that stands between people and their possibilities, usually about two-thirds of the way through a race.

The Wall is not real. It's a concept. It's a metaphor. It's a story. It's a possibility – one of many on any race – but it is not a fact. The Wall only exists in people's minds.

Even though I felt like the world's biggest fraud sitting up there, having an existential crisis about my very purpose on earth and wanting the panel to be over as quickly as possible so I could have another fucking drink, something about this question floored me. It floored me because I suddenly saw it from the other side. This girl looked terrified.

Instead of focusing on this amazing, exciting day she had coming up, a day she had prepared for and dreamt about for months, instead of planning how she would feel having completed 13.1 miles for the first time, instead of celebrating the result of all that training, all she could think about was failing. There was no question in her mind that this Wall existed. The Wall was a given, and it was going to get her. She wanted to know where it was and what it would feel like. It made me so, so sad. I just looked at her, and a message I had clearly needed to tell myself for quite some time came out of my mouth from nowhere.

'The thing is,' I said to her, 'there is no wall.'

I only registered what I was saying as the words left my mouth. Here was I, sitting on a stool like a robot. Capable, honest, inspiring Allie. That's what people saw. That is not what was going on. There was nothing going on. I was a fucking mess. It was only when this girl asked that question that my brain switched on. I was sitting there on that stool facing my own massive wall. Allie the ultrarunner, mental health campaigner, adventurer, all-round fun-times gal. That's what people had come to see. But what *I* saw was Allie the anxious alcoholic; a failing, pathetic, unloveable fuck-up. Allie the mess. Allie the fraud. I was surrounded by my own wall, that I had created with my own mind. A wall that I had built brick by brick over the past two decades. A wall that I was *convinced* was there. A wall that was a lie. Imaginary. And this girl had just made me realise that, or at least say it out loud for the first time.

There was absolutely nothing stopping this girl from having a blinder of a half-marathon except the stories she was telling herself about this Wall. There was nothing stopping me from having a blinder of a life except the stories I was telling myself about mine. I will never forget that day. It was a lightning bolt moment of realisation. It was an awakening. An awakening that would take years to unravel and act on.

There Is No Wall.

PART ONE
THE AWAKENINGS

BLOG EXCERPT: A PROLOGUE TO MADNESS

Published 17 October 2017
Age: 36
Years drinking: 22
Years running: 9
Listen to: 'Footshooter' – Frightened Rabbit

I can't honestly remember the last time I was truly happy. I don't actually believe this happiness exists. As humans, we need to suffer to understand what it is to love and to be joyful. It's just with some of us, the suffering presides over everything else. It's an overarching numbness that is almost impossible to explain. In the last six months, I have been fighting with myself more than I usually do. There have been events that have tilted and knocked me, and helped me to prove to myself what a worthless individual I am. There have been moments of utter confusion and despair within social occasions I should have been enjoying. There have been many, many moments when I have truly wanted to disappear, and sometimes physically have. There have been evenings where I have drunk myself away from the noise in my head to the point of blackout. And there have been very real thoughts of suicide and very real episodes of self-harm. There have been a few hours of clarity when I have decided to get on with what I have had to do that day, and there have been days where I have actually been OK. But there have been many more days where I haven't been OK at all. This story doesn't start on 10 October 2017. It starts a lot longer ago than that.

I had been in the throes of an episode of depression for about three weeks before 'the thing' happened. I hadn't slept much. I had been ill, a slight cold, something that looking back may have been a sign to stop. I had attended a few social gatherings I couldn't cope with. I had got blackout drunk and screamed at two of my closest friends. I was behaving increasingly irrationally, and I couldn't see any further than the next minute. I had slashed at my legs with a pair of scissors and counted how many painkillers I had in the house. I had googled how many it would take for me not to wake up. I didn't have enough.

I had run a really bad marathon the Sunday before. It was bad because I was exhausted and hungover. I had been kept awake the night before the race by suicidal thoughts; hallucinations of me rigging up a ligature in the bedroom I was staying in. I had stood at the edge of the road and thought about throwing myself in front of the cars. I had stood at the edge of the Underground platform and thought about throwing myself in front of a train. I was completely terrified of myself. I was a danger to myself. I was walking through treacle and trying to pretend that this would pass. It always passes. But then it comes back. I am scared that one day I won't come back.

10 October 2017

Today was the day. It was the day I had a full-on breakdown, the breakdown that I would actually take notice of, because the ones before had been numbed and ignored and poked into the inside pocket of my outdoor coat for years. This one was twenty-odd years in the making. I was on Tottenham Court Road. I went looking for some pillows, because the pillows on my bed had felt like they were made of stones the night before when I couldn't sleep, between terrors. They felt like stones on my hands and also in my mouth, but I hadn't bitten them. It just felt like that on the inside of my mouth, and I could taste blood. Between the terrors. But every time I went in a shop, I was overwhelmed by pillows and types of pillows. I want the pillows you get in the hotels. Not the duck down ones, the really firm ones that are also duck down but also something else. And also, there were people; normal, happy people and couples, really middle-class ones who were very attractive and happy and had worked hard to be that attractive and happy, and they were feathering their nests and making a home, and I wanted to kill them and be them at the same time.

When I left the shops without pillows, I stood on Tottenham Court Road and I started to cry. I couldn't understand why, and I couldn't stop crying. Or I would stop crying, but then about a minute later it would start again. I couldn't work out where I was or what I was doing. I got on the Tube, still crying. The Tube was packed. Nobody said anything. I got off the train and went to the pub. In the pub, I wrote the words below. Because this is how I felt. I haven't edited these words. This is how I felt.

I am living in fear of myself. I want to hurt myself. I think about it every day, maybe eight or nine times a day. I watch the cars and the trains. I have a whole drawer of codeine. I have self-harmed with scissors, something I haven't done for eighteen years. I cut my legs. The things I rely on to run. I have looked on the internet for anything I can take that will make me fall asleep and not wake up but has to be 100%, no accidents or pain or anything. I go in food shops and cannot make a decision about what to buy, so I buy nothing and go home hungry and just drink wine. I go into other shops and spend £60 on stuff I don't need, and I don't know why. I buy things on Amazon. Lots of things.

I go into catatonic states of staring at nothing; I miss my stop multiple times in life on the bus and in my brain. I go to the pub and sit there for three hours on my own because I am afraid to go home because I don't want my housemates to see me or talk to me because they are probably going to tell me to move out because I am so fucked up. I have night terrors and can't sleep. I am always tired, and I always have a headache. I hallucinate that I am setting up ligatures in my bedroom, that a white snake is trying to bite my face; I physically jump away from imaginary things like the snake, to wake myself, but I am not asleep. Lots of times, when I have to speak to a person in a shop or in the world outside my bedroom, the world that I have become so afraid of, I pretend to be on a phone call so I won't have to look at them and can just say, 'Sorry, hang on', and then mutter what I want at the shop or outside person, and carry on my fake phone call, not look them in the eye and walk away with my useless purchase.

Sometimes I feel a manic push to be kind, and then I ask people around me if they are OK – one person after another for a whole morning – on the Tube usually, and also when I am running a marathon or something, and it makes me feel amazing for a minute.

Sometimes I feel a calmness that I know is the feeling that some people get shortly before they commit suicide. I know because I have tried to commit suicide before. The thing I feel the most though is fear, in my heart and in my stomach, and that's all the time really. I don't know what I am scared of, but I am fucking terrified. It's next-level fear.

And to my friends, this. I don't reply to your texts, and I hate our WhatsApp groups and I want to leave all of them, so I don't reply. You make me angry, and I don't care. I am really glad you're all having such a fucking easy, funny, nice life. I can't concentrate. I am not part of your group any more because I am different. I am damaged. I'm not who I pretended to be when I first joined the group. This is the real me. The person who hates people who are happy. I really do. I fucking HATE couples. I hate them, and wish they were dead or would cheat on each other and both find out because that's fucking life.

I don't want to go for a drink or coffee or a run or a catch-up or a talk or vent or whatever language you put it in, I want to vanish. I am vicious. You didn't contact me before someone told you they thought something might be wrong, and so don't fucking contact me now. You can't 'cheer me up'. Things you say make me cringe, and you're lying that it's not a burden, because it is. I am carrying it around and it is killing me. It is a burden. I'll prove it's a burden, when you either stop talking to me because you're so bored of what a fucking idiot I am, or I fucking top myself.

I don't believe the things you say when I drunkenly manage

to tell you that I am scared I might kill myself, or I cry at nothing. Don't fucking touch me. I come home shitfaced for four days in a row because the only thing that shuts the howling in my head and the clawing in my stomach is alcohol, and for a while I can sleep without terror. I don't deserve any help, but I so desperately want it, but I don't know what help I need. I should be able to control this because I am a thirty-six-year-old woman who owns her own business, who runs ultramarathons, and whose holiday looked GREAT on Instagram.

This is so embarrassing.

I wish I was covered in scales, or it came up in a rash or was a tumour so you could see it. I've gone a few days without alcohol; maybe it's that? It's not. It's me.

I pretend to be OK all the time. I can do this very well in the mornings, but in the afternoons when I am tired, something takes over that I can't control. I am losing the ability to communicate. I forget words and sentences and names. I have no patience. I can still put on a show, but in the afternoons crying starts without warning; this happens a lot, and then I stop it and then it starts again and I try to stop it but can't, and I decide if someone asks me if I am OK on the Tube or when I am in the pub drinking and hiding, I will say, 'Yes, I am fine, my dog just died', and do a smile, but nobody ever really asks, and I don't have a dog. And on it goes.

I have completely lost grip on reality in this sense. I am living day to day. My work half gets done. My meetings get done. My afternoons are blurred, but they get done. When I get home, sometimes I see my housemate and she is so kind. She is kind because she has been here before when I tried to kill myself, but there is nothing she can do, and she knows it. Sometimes I am a fucking cunt to her, when I am drunk. We don't talk about these times the next day. I go in my room and shut the door, and nobody bothers me.

When I have finished writing this down in the pub, I go home and I am shaky and fogged by wine and no dinner. I am numb. I don't feel hungry. My housemates ask me if I am OK. I say no and I go straight to bed. I think the reality of the situation will frighten them. I set my alarm for 8 a.m. to call the doctor. I need to see a doctor. Today is World Mental Health Day.

CHAPTER 1
WHAT THE FUCK HAPPENED?

Listen to: 'These Are the Days of Our Lives' – Queen

Reading that blog back now is painful. Super fucking painful. It makes me wince. There are parts of it that I don't remember happening, and, at the time of writing, it was only six years ago. This was the first time I had properly documented what happened when I got really ill. It doesn't mean it was the first time it had happened, and it certainly wasn't the last. It actually feels like it happened to someone else, but it happened to me. I wrote those words in real time, and this was not even pre-running me. It was running me. I had been running for about nine years at this point and was about to take on my first 100-miler. Running hadn't saved me. Not by a long way. But credit where it's due, it had definitely gone some way to keeping me alive.

I did see a doctor. She didn't know what to do with me, sent a prescription for antidepressants, that I had neither agreed to take nor approved, to Boots in Hackney, and then told me to go and pick them up. She also gave me the number for the mental health crisis helpline in case I felt like killing myself. An hour later, when I felt like killing myself, I phoned the number, and it was wrong. To cut a long story short, I ended up in crisis care. I went back to my mum's in Dorset, where I stayed for less than a week before coming back to London and starting where I had left off before running my first 100-mile race.

Although I don't remember some of the experiences documented here in full technicolour, I will never, ever forget the pain. It's a pain I've felt in the years since and sometimes feel now. It scares the shit out of me. It's devastating, it's crippling, and it was something that had built within me in the years preceding this breakdown, like a cancer. The fear, the futility, the shame, the anger, the despair and the feeling of never-ending utter hopelessness. You get the picture. When I feel it starting now, it's like a pilot light going on. A recognisable whoosh followed by a tiny raging flame in the pit of my stomach or sometimes the top of my chest. It's a pain that opens the door to all sorts of thoughts and behaviours that I sometimes think are long gone and that I never want to have to live with again. The difference is that now I have the tools to be able to extinguish that flame and they work about eighty per cent of the time. When they don't, I ask for help. Or at least try to.

As well as being my first documented breakdown, this was also the first time I had attempted to get some actual professional help while in the trenches with it. I'd been on and off drugs and in and out of therapy for years, but this was the first 'help me, I think I am going to die' moment. I'd had about six months of these intense, hellish feelings prior to the events of October 2017, but in reality, that day was years and years in the making. At the time I thought it was my rock bottom. It had to be. It was not.

It was the latest and loudest in a long line of alarm bells – ones that told me to change something, anything, to try to live a life instead of simply existing in misery. And I did want to change something. I wanted to change who I was. I wanted to be anyone but myself. I absolutely refused to accept the situation, to accept I was severely ill or that I had a problem with my own concept of self-worth. I point-blank refused to accept that I may have had a bit of a troublesome relationship with alcohol either. I just wanted 'it' to be gone.

Prior to this breakdown, I had spent decades trying to be someone, anyone, but Alice Hannah Bailey. As hard as I tried, I couldn't hide from myself forever, but I gave it a fucking good go. It had become second nature to pretend, and it wouldn't be until six years later that I actually understood this. Let me give you a bit of background on the great pretending game. Let me try to explain how it had got to this point. It started when I was eleven or twelve. It went on for twenty-nine years.

You'll be thrilled to know that my childhood sob story is no worse than anyone else's. I grew up in a family of seven. My mum, dad, three brothers and a sister. My little brothers, Jack and Olly, were very slightly younger than me – a year and two years respectively. My older brother, Tom, and my sister, Janey, were a lot older – ten and eleven years. Technically they're my half-siblings, but we lived together our entire childhoods and I never clocked the fact we had a different dad until someone said it at school when I was about ten. In my eyes they will always be my true brother and sister. Poor fuckers had to bring us up while trying to be cool kids in the 1980s – something that to this day they won't let us forget. There is nothing less sexy for any teenager (let alone one that grew up in the 1980s) than having three siblings under the age of four.

Home was fine. It was fine. It was stressful, noisy and full, and we had no money. There were some pretty strict rules in place – there have to be when you have a small army in the house – but we were very loved. I was the apple of my dad's eye. He treated me like his only daughter, and we were thick as thieves. I got away with murder with him. I absolutely adored him. I would do anything for him. My brilliant, funny, clever dad. Of course, I loved my mum too, but she always seemed a bit stressed and sad; Dad was usually way more fun. He was very charismatic. We would sit in the little conservatory at the back of the house listening to records and talking about The Beatles and Elton John. I was his little Dolly Dewdrop. That's what he called me. I idolised him.

You did what you were told in that house. You always helped and you didn't fuck about. There were consequences if you did. We all had a pretty heavy work ethic drilled into us. You didn't make a fuss, you didn't seek attention, you just got on with it. You helped, you shared, you were honest, and you worked as a team. In hindsight, there were some pretty bad examples of 1980s and 1990s parenting around this time. If you did something wrong, you were punished (sometimes physically). Emotions weren't really things that were encouraged unless they were good, fun ones, and alcohol was an integral part of life. Alcohol meant fun in our house.

Threats were a commonly used parenting technique, and included but weren't limited to: threatening to call social services to take us away, threatening to call the police to take us away/report a minor crime that one of us had committed (usually stealing food), threatening to tell the other parent what shits we were, or threatening us with a 'smack'. This was 1980s parenting at its best. While we were all very loved, the rules were the rules. My brothers tended to push back more than I did, and my older brother and sister moved out the minute they could. It was around that point things started to change.

When I was eleven, I passed the eleven-plus, a 'standardisation' exam that aims to tell you exactly how clever your eleven-year-old is. It was an idea conceived and popularised in the 1940s – around the same time that it was decided that smoking was good for you and women should distract toddlers from fireplaces by getting them to play with an ashtray. Passing that test was an accident. I was not academically gifted in any way. I could write a really good story and I loved a bit of drama, but I wasn't a standout child by any stretch. My dad was over the moon. He informed me I was to go to Bournemouth School for Girls. I didn't know what that was. I wanted to go to the school my older brother and sister had gone to – the one you could walk to up the road. Bournemouth School for Girls was a girls-only grammar school and was also a forty-five-minute bus ride away. I'd have to get a bus, on my own, every day. I didn't want to go. I vocalised this. It became apparent that it was non-negotiable. I remember my dad saying that some of his friends had 'paid' to get their daughters in, so I was very, very lucky. What I *actually* was, was fucking terrified.

My uniform was second-hand and too big. I had second-hand books and only one jacket – the one I wore when I occasionally got to go horse riding. It was an oversize wax jacket that smelt like the stables. None of my junior school friends were going to this school. They stopped talking to me because I was 'going to the posh school'. The class divide was real in my eleven-year-old world.

Picture this. First week at said school, I tried to make friends with a girl who I really liked. She rode horses too, but at the expensive stables and she didn't have to muck them out first. It was her birthday during the first week of term and I wanted to get her a gift, but I didn't have any money. I went home and got my favourite book about horses and brought it in, wrapped up in tin foil, and presented it to her at lunchtime in front of all the other girls. I was really excited; I knew she would love it and we would be best friends.

It was a big book with lots of pictures of different breeds of horses in it. I would sometimes trace the horse on the front cover using a pencil and tracing paper. I wasn't very good at drawing, so thought if I traced the pictures I would get better at it. I had traced these horses *a lot*. This had left indents in the cover and on most of the pages, but it was my favourite book and I wanted to give it to her. Sharing things is kind. I'd been taught that at home. And I wanted her to be my friend. My mum and I bought most of my clothes from charity shops, so second-hand was good. Second-hand was normal.

When she opened it, she just stared at it, then stared at me in horror and said, 'Is this second-hand? That is SO SKANKY', and started laughing. Everyone else started laughing too. Using the word 'skanky' was one of the most vicious acts of public shaming available to eleven-year-old girls in the early 1990s. I was so humiliated. I couldn't understand why she was being so horrible. It was a book I loved, and I had been trying to be kind. It was hideous. She left it on the desk and walked off. And my fate was sealed. From that day on, it was war at school. I never fought back. I just put my head down and got on with it. That's how I eventually did get clever.

I quickly learnt that you can't get bullied if you spend all your time in the library – people have to be quiet in the library – so I spent the first three years of secondary school there. I was getting that great education my dad had wanted while being so intensely miserable and fearful that I can't even begin to describe it on these pages. Maybe that was his plan all along?

The library was one thing, the corridors and classrooms were another. I just learnt to take it on the chin. It was fucking awful. Name-calling, passive-aggressive comments, trusting nobody, a panic attack brewing as I ran the gauntlet of the science corridor, all the usual stuff. I told nobody. My mum had an idea, but not of the scale. The years went on – Year 7, 8, 9. I went through periods of being OK, but my friendships never lasted. My financial situation was very different to everyone else's, and it showed all the time. I never told my dad how I felt. He'd become prone to shouting a lot at home, and I knew his opinion anyway. I needed to work harder to catch up with the other girls.

My mum didn't come to my first parents' evening. I don't know why. My dad did. I don't remember the conversations that took place with the teachers, but I remember the car journey home. I remember the smell of the car, I remember the mood in the car, and I remember him telling me that I needed to be better at English, Science and Maths. I needed to work really hard to catch up with the other girls. I needed to be better at everything.

I'm sure he remembers this as a bit of encouraging conversation. I remember it as being told I wasn't enough. I remember it as being told I had let him down. I remember the feeling of utter deflation as we drove through the school gates after a one-way conversation that formed one of the cornerstones of my life. A feeling of total disappointment in myself. I had let down the man I loved, simply by being me. I was not enough as I was. Fade to black.

It was around this time that I consciously decided that I didn't want to be me at all. The girls at school didn't like me, my dad was disappointed in me, my brothers seemed to hate me, and I really didn't like myself. At school we were always pushed to be better or the best, and if you weren't good at something they simply stopped you doing it and made you do something else. That's why I never did PE and am terrified of maths. The only thing I was good at was English, and hiding in the library. I wasn't getting any exercise at school or being encouraged to do it. I never got picked for the school sports teams, and the netball court may as well have been a San Antonio prison yard. My brothers were in local football teams so got out at weekends, and I very, very occasionally rode horses, but that was literally it. And it stayed that way for twelve years.

At home I hid in my room. When I passed that fucking exam, my parents had bought me a small TV as a reward and I think as a carrot to try to get my younger brothers to do the same. My brothers weren't into carrots. One was into weed and the other was into girls. I spent my after-school time staring at soap operas and American sitcoms and tried to work out how I could be more like the popular girls in *Home and Away* or *Friends*. I changed my name twice – from Alice to Ally to Alicia – and insisted teachers (and my parents) always used my new name. While my peers all went to netball practice or hung around in groups on the field at lunchtime, I hid in my library sanctuary. Non-school-uniform days were the *worst* days of my life. They all came in wearing Topshop and New Look; I was in whatever my sister had grown out of. I vividly remember scavenging an old River Island bag out of a bin and walking around with my school folder in it, hoping the other girls would think that was where I shopped. But they knew I had got it out of the bin because it smelt of oranges and bin juice. They took the piss even more.

I joined the school band hoping to be asked to play the flute. We couldn't afford a flute, so I had to play the cornet, mainly because we had one in the loft. That stint was short-lived. Overall, in Years 7–9, I did no sport, joined no clubs, had no friends. Saying that, my Year 7 PE report does state: 'Alice shows a little promise as a runner, if only she could apply herself.' To be fair, it would probably read the same now.

Anyone but me. I just wanted to be anyone but me. And then my world properly imploded.

My parents had been at each other's throats for a while – some low-level dinner-time plate-smashing and shouting. Sometimes I would hide in the cupboard under the stairs to escape the noise. I can still smell it. A mix of piles of ironing, board games and questionable spirits. I felt like there was a distance growing between me and my dad. I'd been caught smoking – ironically introduced to it on a school trip to Alton Towers by the daughter of one of my dad's friends who had 'paid' to get her into that school. I thought being her friend would impress him. Turns out not so much. He wasn't that pleased about it.

I still loved my dad. He was still my world. I would still do anything for him, but it just wasn't the same. I was doing my best at that school for him. He wasn't giving much back. He kept disappearing. You know, for work and stuff. And then one day he was gone.

I don't clearly remember a lot of this period. It devastated me. These are the bits I haven't forgotten and the bits I have managed to fill in. And I haven't forgotten how I felt. Hollow. Just fucking hollow.

A few weeks before it happened there was a lot of shouting and crying in our house. I asked him outright if he was leaving. We were due to go on our first foreign holiday to France, and I was about to turn sixteen. He promised me that he was not leaving, and that he was coming on holiday as planned. And then he didn't. He just didn't come.

When we got back from the World's Worst Holiday™ (the one where my mum drove me and my brothers to France in a Volvo and spent ninety per cent of the time crying or drunk and the other ten per cent driving on the wrong side of the road), there was a letter in the kitchen. All my dad's stuff had gone apart from some of his records. The letter said that he needed some space and had moved into a B&B. It was the day before my sixteenth birthday. They were supposed to buy me a guitar.

At some point we went to the guitar shop. My mum was crying and my dad was acting like nothing was wrong. In fact, he was acting like my mum was being annoying. I just wanted to be somewhere else. I wanted to be someone else. My heart was breaking. At some point when we got home, my mum made him tell me what he'd done. He did tell me what he'd done and, apparently, he was crying about it when he told me. I don't remember the words, but I won't forget staring blankly at him as he sat on the end of my bed. I think that's when I perfected my 'I have no fucking clue what to do with this information' face. There was someone else and he'd moved into her house, not a B&B.

There is nothing wrong with falling out of love with someone and falling in love with someone else. It happens all the time. I get it. That was not the problem. It was the lying that was the problem. What I took from this situation was that he had lied to me and abandoned me. He didn't love me enough to stay. He told me he loved me, he told me he wouldn't leave and then he left me. And that was that.

I spent my sixth-form years being heartbroken, angry and extremely sad while also trying to be cool, liked and pass my A-levels. I'd behaved like an angel the whole time Dad had been around, save the smoking incidents, so fuck it, may as well go full rogue. Or as full rogue as I dared while taking my A-levels. I had an excuse not to fit in at school now. I am from a broken home, I am weird and I like wearing skirts over jeans to school. FUCK YOU ALL.

My rebellion was in fullish swing. I argued with teachers (intelligently, about poetry), I swore a lot, wore terrible make-up, listened to very fucking miserable music, cut my own fringe, drank tequila with the boys on the field and sometimes smoked at school with our overly friendly sociology teacher. I was totally broken-hearted. In my world, the only man I had ever loved had left me. I wrote super-aggrieved poems about it in English, and then got angry when my classmates laughed at me and my teacher questioned me over the prose.

'Fucking CRETINS,' I would muse while indignantly chugging on a Marlboro Light at the bus stop and wishing my dad would come back. Once I flipped a desk in a lesson and walked out. I dyed my hair purple. I stopped talking to anyone that wanted to talk to me. I got into an actual fight with a popular girl at school because I said I thought Michael Jackson's relationships with children were fucking weird, and Jon Bon Jovi was gay, so would never ask her out. A chair was thrown. We had to be separated. I was definitely right about one of those things. I saw myself as super edgy; in reality I was about as edgy as a football. I got very good A-level results.

I stopped taking calls from my dad. Whenever he tried to make contact, I more or less told him to fuck off. I was angry and hurt, and I blamed myself for a lot of it. If I had been cleverer to start off with, or not so annoying, or not so 'bossy' or 'dramatic' (his words, not mine), maybe he would have stayed. I couldn't stop thinking that maybe me not measuring up had made him embarrassed. I couldn't stop thinking that if I'd been someone else completely, maybe he wouldn't have gone at all.

I was in a position at home where I felt like I had to protect my teenage brothers from my mum's utter devastation and protect my mum from my teenage brothers being my teenage brothers. I wanted to please everyone. I wanted to look after everyone. I wanted everyone to love me and nobody to leave me, but I also didn't want to let anyone in at all. I had somewhat miraculously got in with an older crowd outside school and would go with them to nightclubs that played rock and indie music at the weekends. Sometimes I would go during the week. 'Studying at Natalie's' was what I called it. Natalie was a new friend who had joined sixth form, and her mum was an art teacher at the college in town, so was pretty free and loose with the rules. It was great. I started drinking most weekends and sometimes during the week. I felt like I fitted in with those people in those clubs. I fitted in when I was drunk. We all fit in when we're drunk.

From the outside I imagine it looked like everything was relatively OK and I was doing normal teenage stuff. Smoking, drinking, being moody all the time. But something inside me hurt. My heart felt like it hurt. I felt very lost. I felt very lonely. I felt like I wasn't really in my body most of the time. I didn't really understand emotions, because every time I showed emotion, I was told I was being dramatic. The classic lines in my house were, 'If you've got nothing nice to say then don't say anything at all', and, 'Stop moaning.' I didn't really talk to anyone about it. I just festered, marinating in my own self-loathing, anxiety and fear that if I did tell anyone, they would abandon me as a friend, a sister, a daughter.

I lost my virginity when I was sixteen to a person who looked like a young Mick Jagger, was about eight years older than me and had a pretty tasty drug habit that I was, at the time, unaware of. He drove a Triumph Dolomite and collected vintage suitcases. He was, by all accounts, a total knob. He dumped me at about 1 a.m. in a nightclub, when he had run out of drugs and I had run out of money to give him.

Once I got over this person (mainly by sitting on my windowsill listening to The Verve and crying a lot), I developed a habit of sleeping with any member of the opposite sex that showed even the remotest interest in me. This was obviously easiest done when drunk and would, I romanticised, lead to love and a lasting relationship because boys like girls who have sex with them. That logic didn't work out brilliantly for me, or anyone else ever as far as I know.

Every time someone ghosted me post-terrible shag, I thought it was because I wasn't thin enough, pretty enough, cool enough or clever enough. It might *actually* have been because they were teenage boys and, like sharks, they would go for the most vulnerable, easy option to get what they wanted. I just happened to be there. I was getting a reputation as someone that would have sex with pretty much anyone with little to no consequences. I repeated the same behaviour over and over again, hoping for a different outcome, but oddly getting the same outcome every single time. It was like a really gross, miserable version of *Groundhog Day*. For a time, I convinced myself that I was actually a proper feminist: I was using *them*, doing what *I* wanted with *my* body – a proper boss move. In reality, I was dying on the inside. I was desperate for approval and love no matter what form it took.

At the end of my A-levels, I decided to move to London. I decided I was going to work in the music industry. I responsibly ran away from all the mess at home by going to university.

I remember telling my dad where I was going on the phone. My dad told me that I should be studying law at Southampton where he was working, so he could 'keep an eye on me'. Once again, I pretty much told him to fuck off. He told me the degree I had chosen was a Mickey Mouse degree and it would get me nowhere. Turns out it was a Mickey Mouse degree and it kind of got me nowhere. He could still fuck off, though.

I enrolled at Goldsmiths, University of London, to study media and communications a couple of weeks before I turned eighteen, an angry, frustrated, always hungover and extremely insecure mess. I cried when my mum dropped me off. My brother jumped out of the car as they were pulling away and passed me a Werther's Original through the window of my tiny room. I cried and cried and cried. Then I ate the Werther's Original. And then I started my professional drinking career. I could do whatever the fuck I wanted at university. And I did.

We've touched on the drinking at home when I was growing up. It's probably important to revisit it now. The drinking thing had started in my teens like it does with everyone: an illicit beer here and there, a stolen bottle of red wine complete with pink vomit in the garden, sipping from the bottles in the cupboard under the stairs and filling them up with water. All the classics. My parents were pretty lax with it; they let us drink little beers from about the age of fourteen – my mum's classic, 'Well, if you're doing it at home, you're not doing it on a street corner.' Mum, we were doing it at home *and* on a street corner.

Once the drinking started, it never actually stopped. Historically, my parents drank 'socially'. Socially in the 1980s and 1990s meant everywhere, all the time, because it was normal. The pub car park was my second home. The pub garden became my third. There were a lot of drunken evenings in my family home, but the majority of them were filled with laughter and silliness, not fighting or horror. My parents were fun and relaxed and loved each other when they were drunk. It was when they weren't that it was a problem.

At university I found it easiest to break the ice with people by getting drunk and/or sleeping with them, and here, there was nobody to even attempt to rein in my behaviour. In fact, everyone just encouraged it.

I did my university 'work' while holding down a part-time job and a full-time drinking habit. I drank at least six pints of lager a day topped off with a massive bowl of nachos. That was my diet for about three years. It was normal. It was social. I was super rock and roll, living the London life with my part-time job at Our Price in Lewisham, my credit card and my fake leather jacket. I went out to super-dodgy bars, hung out with super-dodgy people and did super-dodgy things. I wrote my dissertation on David Bowie; I went to loads and loads and loads of gigs. I DJ'ed badly in the students' union. I spent money I did not have (God I *loved* my cheque book).

While I had no intention of being in a band, I had every intention of sleeping with *anyone* in a band. And I did. Loads of them. I got a boyfriend who was not only a lot older than me but also a cocaine addict. Bingo! I broke his leg pushing him out of a window when I was drunk and he was high.

In my second year, I tried to kill myself. I was, once again, super drunk. I cut my wrists, the wrong way, with a razor. I do remember thinking, *For fuck's sake, Allie, you can't even do that right*. I tried to hide what I had done by wearing sweatbands, but my housemate (and new best friend, Cat) found out and marched me to the university doctor. This would not be the last time Cat had to get me out of this situation. The university doctor put me on antidepressants and made me go and see the university therapist. It was a classic therapy experience. A table with a box of tissues and a sympathetic head-nodding woman who kept saying the words 'low mood'. She asked if I wanted to talk about my dad, and guess what? I told her to fuck off. That was the end of that. I carried on as before.

I somehow got through university with a 2:1 and continued to work at Our Price for a year after graduating. I wanted to work in the music industry and thought this was my way in – selling 99p cassettes to the Lewisham massive. I had wanted to work in music since the age of fourteen. I had been told many, many times this was a pipe dream, by my school, my parents, my mates and some of my university lecturers. I had *no idea* how to break into music, and sleeping with members of low-level shit indie bands/working in Our Price hadn't worked to this point. I naively thought that on graduation day I would be swept off my feet by one of the big record companies. Why did I think this? Because Blur had gone to Goldsmiths. Another brilliant piece of logic.

I wasn't swept off my feet on graduation day; I had no idea what I was going to do with my life, so I kept working at Our Price, pretending I was still a student and munching my way through overdraft after overdraft after overdraft. Maybe my twenties would be better? (Narrator: They would not be better.)

After university I was plunged into what I now call the lost years. My twenties were ridiculous. I did so much, but I also did absolutely fuck all. I don't really remember my mental state in any detail during this period because I was drunk for all of it. Don't remember much of what happened, haven't forgotten the pain.

I know I spent a lot of time fighting against myself. My depression continued unmonitored. My experience with the university doctor had put me off seeking any more help. I fucking *hated* myself eighty per cent of the time. It wasn't all abject misery, there were some pretty hilarious good times, but everything was tinged with this emptiness, a sort of lack of understanding or focus or ambition – a heaviness like I was desperately trying to get to the end of something. I didn't know what was wrong with me. Everyone else seemed fine.

There were a number of very serious drink-related incidents around this time, things like the police being called when I went missing after a night out (I was found unconscious on a night bus); more drunken attempts on my own life; shitting myself on the doorstep of my own house more than once; spending nights passed out in taxi ranks, bus stations, at the end of Tube lines; waking up in a cupboard in a house in Cirencester; losing multiple phones and wallets (mine and other people's); losing house keys and car keys (mine and other people's); waking up in a gravel pit in East London; accidentally smoking opium thinking it was a cigarette; having a loaded gun held to my head in a pub; muggings shrugged off, assaults shrugged off; accidentally getting married. The list goes on. I found myself in numerous situations that were extremely chaotic and incredibly dangerous.

Back then, I thought it was rock and roll; now I see it was fucking stupid. I hung around with some absolute wasters. They liked me because I was a people-pleaser and wanted to be loved, so I would give them things like money, guitars and blow jobs. I was actually extremely vulnerable. I told myself that these were the people I *should* be hanging around with. These were the ones with the music industry contacts. They were also the ones with things written on their living room wall in human blood, dirty needles all over their house, the occasional lingering arrest warrant hanging round their neck and human shit in their bath.

Behind that grotty glamour that occasionally made me feel OK, the heaviness loomed. Everything was so fucking hard. The depression was getting worse and I was trying to ignore it. I had literally compressed all my feelings, emotions and fears from school and university into a place in my body where they could not get out or wriggle about. When they did try to get out or wriggle about, I would drink and they would be quiet. That meant I was drinking most of the time. Something will happen, I used to tell myself. Something will happen and then you'll be happy.

It doesn't work like that.

I got married in July 2004. I did love my future ex-husband, in the way you love someone in your early twenties, when you're drunk. I remember sitting there, on my wedding day, in the registry office in Poole thinking, *This is not a good idea.* Turns out it was not a good idea. The wedding was arranged in just under two weeks and cost a total of £400. I had been with him for about two years. This was the final option. I was a people-pleaser. I wanted him to be the one. Plus, if he was married to me, he couldn't abandon me. Not easily anyway. I didn't think about what would happen if I needed to abandon him.

The marriage lasted four years on and another five years off. I felt like I knew he was cheating on me but he denied it. It broke me. I added it to the list of reasons I knew I was unloveable. I concluded it was my fault. I stuck at it. Sometimes we were happy – as happy as you can be with no money, a drink and drugs problem and zero trust. We went to Glastonbury every single year. We lived in some of the worst flats in Whitechapel. We spent *all* our money on records and booze. I was drinking or hungover most days; he was on a comedown. It was totally normal. We started a fanzine that was extremely short-lived. I got temping jobs working in administrative roles for the DFES and Natural History Museum; he got a job managing a shop. The plan was to get 'good' as a personal assistant and get into the music industry that way. My twenties were mayhem. At best chaotic, at worst a car crash. But I did achieve one thing. I got that dream job. I fucking did it.

My relationship with the future ex-husband had got weirder and weirder. I felt like he was becoming more controlling. He hated it when I started working in music. He didn't like me going out or staying out, and he didn't like me having friends at work. I did everything I could to try to make that marriage work; in the first few years I was a pretty good wife in the 1950s sense of the word. But when I got my music job, I took my eye totally off that ball. I had a bigger and more shiny ball to play with. I had achieved my dream, and I sort of assumed he would support me. On the night that I was told I got the job (after seven years of applying to every major label and being constantly knocked back), I just remember him being really quiet.

His behaviour became more and more erratic. The mind games started. I didn't want to upset him, but I was also extremely uncomfortable with how things were going. At one point I drunkenly threatened to leave him. He responded by telling me that I could never leave him. *Hold my fucking beer*, I thought. *Nobody puts Bailey in a corner*.

I ended our marriage by attempting to have an affair with someone I worked with. This person had shown a mild interest in me that I mistook for *actual* interest, and within about a week, love – not just no-strings-attached sex, which is what it actually was. I made sure my future ex-husband found out. I would not recommend this method of ending a marriage. What a cunty thing to do, right?

Cheating on someone is fucking horrible, but I did it. I'd seen it work before with my parents. In this case, it was out of desperation more than anything else. When my future ex-husband found out what I had done, he very calmly told me to tell everyone we knew that ending it was by 'mutual decision'. So I did. I pretty much always did what he said. Until I didn't any more. Getting that job had made me brave; for a while I felt invincible, for a while I felt like I was enough, and I wasn't having someone tell me what to do. I'd love to say I was gutted when we split up, but I was just relieved. Now I could do anything I wanted.

Enter the Music Industry.

CHAPTER 2
YOU ARE SO LUCKY

Listen to: 'You Don't Know How Lucky You Are' – Keaton Henson

I cannot explain in words how much I love music. I just can't. I feel like it's in my blood. I've loved it since I can remember, and I still love it now. It was probably listening to those records in the conservatory with my dad when I was eleven or twelve that really did it. Music had the power to make me feel different: calm and understood, excited and hopeful or empowered. I suppose it made me feel as much like myself as I could when I was growing up, even if just for the moments I was listening to it. Later in my teens it brought me together with like-minded people. In the clubs we could dance to the same beat, and in those moments, I didn't have to pretend to be someone else. I could just be me. We all had a shared interest, a shared love. I sometimes think that now about running events. They're a lot like music festivals. Everyone there for the same thing, no bullshit, no who is coolest or who earns the most money or has the best job, just the adventure. We are all there running together like we are all there singing together. It's an incredible thing.

The thing that got me about music was the lyrics. I loved the idea that other people suffered like I did: not liking who they were, not understanding their situation, being broken-hearted, being angry, being an outsider. They made me feel seen and understood. If I got into a band, I really got into them. I read everything I could get my hands on: books, magazines, papers. I borrowed CDs from the library. I recorded the charts off the radio. I joined the Britannia Music Club (remember that?). I recorded every *Top of the Pops* I could, and I'd watch the clips over and over again. I learnt everything there was to know about the various subcultures I identified with: mods, rockers, punks, goths, indie kids, townies. I went through a period in my late teens of only listening to stuff from the 1960s and only wearing clothes from that time. I made my mum backcomb my hair and put false eyelashes on me. I spent all my money on CDs and vinyl. My first gig – don't laugh – was Take That at Wembley Arena in 1994. My sister took me. I was completely mesmerised. When Take That split up (the darkest day), I moved on to Blur and Oasis – still boy bands but cool ones with guitars and swear words. Unpopular opinion: Blur and Oasis were as much boy bands as Westlife and Boyzone were and would never have been as successful as they were had Take That not split up. Think about it.

When I was fifteen, I started writing gig reviews for the local paper in the hope I would get free tickets for stuff. I went to see bands whenever I could. I worked every summer in shitty pubs to make enough money to go to my first Glastonbury Festival – an ill-advised adult-free trip that ended up with my mum having to buy a ticket to come and rescue me from a flooded tent in 1998. She didn't come and march me home. She just brought some fresh sleeping bags and sandwiches, watched Robbie Williams and then left. I think that was the day that my mum went from being just my mum to being my all-time hero.

I was music obsessed. After an incredibly embarrassing two-week stint as lead singer of the world's worst indie band when I was sixteen, I decided behind the scenes might be best for me. I read an article in *Smash Hits* about a girl who was the press officer for East 17. I had no idea what a press officer was, but I knew who East 17 were. In hindsight she must have really had her work cut out. Anyway, I wanted to be her. I didn't want to be me doing her job. I wanted to be her. It all seemed so glamorous and exciting. It was out of this world. It was out of my world. If I could get into the music industry, I reasoned, I could be someone else. Everything would be magically OK. My mind would be fixed, I would be cool and liked, my hair would suddenly look great, I'd get a real leather jacket and I would be enough. A record label is where I would become that mythical confident, cool, happy person. That is where I would grow into someone I liked and everyone else loved. I would have the dream life. It all seemed so simple. Except it didn't actually work out like that.

Like any exciting romance, music starts off with glamour and parties and drinks and doing well. The good times. It starts off by telling you that you are great and beautiful and glamorous and loved, and you have made it and you are the best. But if you are a vulnerable people-pleaser (I was), if you don't maintain boundaries (I had none), if you are even a little bit insecure (erm ...) and if you really struggle with the idea of feeling like you are worth anything, the music industry will slowly start to control you. And if you let it, it will destroy you.

You don't notice it at first, but it becomes your life, your identity and your only love. You start to only have time for it. Nothing else. It's exciting and shiny and new. It's what you've always wanted. You throw everything you have at it. Your old friends fade into nothing and your family starts failing to register as a priority at all; the industry becomes your family. It is cult-like. If you're not built for it, if you're not aware of what is going on, it will start to pull you down. That goes for both artists and label employees. I spent eleven years begging for the job I loved to love me back and doing anything I could to keep it in my life.

I was twenty-seven when I started working at my first label. Before I got that job, I had applied to, and been rejected by, every major label in the UK. Twice. It took seven years of applying to finally get that acceptance. I am still, to this day, extremely proud of myself for sticking with it. But I am also a bit confused as to why I did stick with it. Even with people telling me it was stupid or a dream, I never gave up. I find it incredibly hard to understand this, even now. I honestly believed I was born to do it and it would happen, despite actual evidence to the contrary coming in the post every few months. Rejection letter after rejection letter. I kept them all for years. Maybe it was the naivety of youth, maybe there was some deep well of grit and drive inside me. Maybe I just really, really like things that are very, very bad for me and very, very hard to do. Ultra-marathons, anyone?

From the first day I swaggered into the reception of my first major label job, I was completely starstruck by what was going on around me. My boss called it 'the dream factory'. I finally had the career I'd wanted since being a teenager. I'd made it. I was here. Everything was going to be OK. I was soooooo lucky. Let's have a drink to celebrate, shall we?

I started as a personal assistant on £17K a year. I had to beg for a ticket to anything, I had to work ridiculous hours, I had to do a massive amount of donkey work, but fuck me did I love it. I loved going to gigs, I loved being in the office, I loved sliding past low-level rappers in the hallway, I loved the stories, the camaraderie, seeing videos and hearing music first. It was a privilege. Sometimes I got to go to parties and meet famous people and get drunk and get a cab home paid for by work. It was what I had always wanted. And people were impressed, my God were they impressed. The external validation was off the scale. I felt like every girl who had ever bullied me back in Bournemouth was now crying into her Pret sandwich. *Ha! This'll show them!* I thought.

However, the hierarchy in record labels at that time was like that of an early Anglo-Saxon settlement. If the execs could have given me buckets of their own shit to carry around and dispose of, I would have been doing it. In fact, I sort of was doing it. I was doing expenses, picking up lunch, delivering dry cleaning, picking up dry cleaning, sorting out tickets, arranging meetings, taking notes in meetings, getting told off when my notes weren't very good and doing anything else that was asked of me. Literally anything. Doctors' appointments for kids, nail appointments for managers, walking dogs for pop stars; every job has its perks. I was happy enough doing it; I would have done anything, and of course I felt like I was treated like shit. I was a nobody in the machine that was the music industry. I had to make a name for myself. I was really lucky to have this job.

Lucky. There's that word. I've used it a few times. Hindsight. There's another word. I'll use that a lot too.

When you work in music, or any of the creative industries, you are constantly told how lucky you are. You are told that there are hundreds of people who would kill for your job. You are told this all the time, every day. It's a control mechanism. You are paid a very low wage which you never question because you get amazing perks like free drinks, gig tickets, free records, aftershow parties and backstage passes. My other free perks included increased low self-esteem, horrendous anxiety, acute paranoia and an exacerbated drinking problem.

I felt like I was expected to work all the time, day or night, and turn a blind eye to certain behaviours. I felt like I was 'lucky' to be there. You have been told that. So you believe it.

Work issued some of us with a BlackBerry. A BlackBerry was absolutely a sign that you were so important and good at your job that you just had to be contactable twenty-four hours a day. This was a good thing, right? Was it bollocks.

We 'hilariously' referred to this device as a CrackBerry, because the addiction to checking it 24/7 was oh so real. After you had received it, plugged it in and charged it, the little red light would start blinking to tell you that you had a message you needed to reply to now. That red light would also suck your very soul out of your body and into the device. Because that fucking thing owned me from the moment I got it to the day I gave it back. It was like a tiny anxiety producer.

I felt like there were no boundaries in music. You are in a boundaryless bubble. I was lucky to have a BlackBerry. I was lucky to be considered important enough to have one. And I was in the lucky position of now being on call 24/7.

I think we have established that it was luck that brought me here. It wasn't that I'd never given up on the dream. It wasn't that I had the endurance to party all night and then come in the next day at 9 a.m. It wasn't that I'd run my own club nights, researched, written letters and applied and applied again for jobs for almost seven years with no joy and kept on fucking doing it. It wasn't that despite people telling me it was a pipe dream, I had pursued it. It wasn't that I'd taken a £10k pay cut from my previous job, sacrificing any notion of financial security or career progression, in order to do this one, and it wasn't that I was actually the perfect candidate for this role: young, creative, hard-working and enthusiastic with an excellent work history, great references and an encyclopaedic knowledge of music. I hadn't been chosen for this job because of that. It wasn't any of that. It was that I was lucky. So fucking lucky. The problem with luck is that it can run out. I was terrified that this would happen and was reminded it could happen at any minute by almost everyone I worked with.

My music career started off super well. The label was very successful, and I was in the honeymoon period, and I had a BlackBerry. But after the first year, things started to feel a bit off. I got a tiny inkling (which I dismissed at the time as imposter syndrome or just being ungrateful) that I wasn't that lucky at all. I had no money and was struggling to pay my rent or eat. It felt like I had a constant rotation of line managers. I wasn't being trained or mentored. I had no idea about career progression, and I wasn't really learning anything – apart from what not to do, how to effectively hide an all-day hangover and that when you're asked to pick up twelve tuna rolls, they mean the sushi variety, not the Tesco bread variety. What a day that was.

I had also been called out at work a few times for some very minor things in what I felt was a very dramatic, unconstructive and public way. In all honesty, about six months in I started to become scared of going to work. I told myself to toughen up. I told myself that I was the person that I had always wanted to be with the slightly more leathery leather jacket and a BlackBerry that, by this point, dictated my every move. I wanted to be right for them. For work. I had developed this slightly-miserable-but-very-funny goth persona that people seemed to like, so I stuck with that. I played that role. I would say and do anything to be liked and accepted, and this was much easier to do when I was drunk. I started to mould my entire personality around a job that I had told myself was 'the dream'. I should be happy by now. But I wasn't. I was anxious. I was lonely. I was on edge and a bit scared of being found out to be completely inadequate and then fired. I was dealing with it in exactly the same way I dealt with romantic relationships. It must be me, I thought, it must be my problem. I am not enough. Must do anything to be enough.

So I continued doing everything I was expected to do to try to become enough. I didn't want to tell anyone how I felt because everyone else was confident and cool and good at what they did. Or I thought they were. I didn't want to tell anyone about the things I saw or heard that I thought were a bit out of order. I remember trying to talk to a couple of people about things I'd witnessed that didn't seem right, but I eventually shut up. I added a hard shell to the misery-goth-girl role, and notched it up a bit, copying behaviours, becoming 'one of the lads'. I would just have to accept this was how it was and ignore the thought that something was wrong. And that was extremely fucking exhausting.

By this point I was 100 per cent indoctrinated into the cult; I unconditionally loved my job. It was my everything and I couldn't imagine doing anything else. It was all-encompassing. I mimicked the behaviour of the successful people without knowing anything about them. I kept my mouth shut when I thought things weren't right or were unfair. I took criticism on the chin. When it hurt, I got drunk. I got heavily involved in the social side of things. I tried to make everyone like me, even though I fucking hated myself. I learnt who not to piss off. I learnt who to avoid on nights out. I learnt what not to say. I never asked questions because I wanted people to think I knew what I was doing – and because I didn't ask questions I would fuck up. There were still times when it was all OK – like, proper OK. There were times where I felt like I had some good friends, I felt like it was working. But like any abusive relationship, any relationship of coercive control, as it felt to me, the good times would be served with a heavy side salad of abhorrent behaviour that was forgiven because of the fact I was scared I would lose my job and so lose my entire identity. My life would be over. Remember how lucky you are, Allie; people would kill for your job.

Sometimes, even writing this now with a clear head, and validation from numerous conversations I've had with ex-colleagues (and the BBC), and even with the public acknowledgement in the form of the #MeToo movement, I sometimes feel like I am making this all up or dramatising it. And that is how abuse works. It makes you feel like it is your fault, or that it didn't really happen, or you are misremembering it. There are things I remember clear as fucking day, and there are bits I can't remember at all, but I will never forget the abject fear of going to work. I will never forget the elephants that stood in every room of that building.

Depression didn't help. Depression and anxiety can amplify the effect of everything as well as making you question everything. It wasn't that bad, it was probably your fault, you were probably shit at your job. That was what I told myself for years. I think it's different now. I know a lot of the labels take the mental health of their employees very seriously, at least on paper. But I spent years thinking on and off that I was shit at my job and being scared to ask for help. It was like a roller coaster. I felt like my life was a cycle of praise and reward, criticism and punishment, and the threat of replacement.

I felt like a number of my peers thrived in this environment, mimicking the behaviour of those further up the ladder. I didn't thrive. Some of us pretended we could handle it and medicated ourselves with drink, drugs or both, to be confident when we knew we were just going to get kicked. I was one of those people. I medicated myself to keep quiet the voice telling me that maybe I had made a mistake. I'd spent seven years at a girls' grammar school, and here I was, back in an environment where I felt like similar behaviour was normalised. But now I was a big girl. There would be no end of term.

My medicine was everywhere – free-flowing and encouraged. Addiction is a plant best kept in a pitch-black room, away from direct sunlight, and it really blossomed in the darkness of the music industry. As time went on and the pressure rose at work – pressure to get things right when you had no idea how to get them right – the anxiety grew. I had a couple of promotions and that made my life worse. Promotion without education. A recipe for disaster. To stop the anxiety, I would drink more often and more heavily. The drink would help for a few hours, then the hangovers would fuel the fear; it would be back with a vengeance the following day. We were encouraged to drink at work. Drinking was rock and roll. Drinks at lunchtime followed by drinks after work, then drinks pre-gig, drinks at gigs, drinks at the show, drinks at the aftershow, one for the road? Shall we go back to the hotel? Drinks at the hotel – oh fuck, it's 3 a.m. and I'm blacked out on some stairs for the third time this week. I would routinely go for a few lunchtime pints before marketing meetings as I had been told I was always more creative after a few beers. Beers before meetings, beers in meetings. Beers in cabs. Beers on the balcony. Round and round we fucking go.

I felt like drinking made me less visible, more likeable and less likely to be spotted and fired for something. I felt like if I didn't drink, I would stick out. I felt like I could melt into the walls after a few drinks. Maybe I felt like this because everyone else was doing it. But was everyone else doing it as much as me? I don't honestly know.

It got to the point where I couldn't actually go out or be social if I wasn't drunk. I encouraged it in others so I wouldn't be the only one. I was the sheepdog, rounding people up to come for pub lunches and after-work drinks. If they didn't come, I would go alone. I could happily be alone and drink, but I could not be alone without drinking.

What with me trying to please everyone at work, do my job, pay my way, manage to not think about topping myself three times a day, maintain an extreme and consistent drinking habit, and with my ill-advised marriage coming to a car-crash ending, I slowly but surely became not just ill, but very, very ill. I thought that my depression would be cured by getting a nice new job. How could I be depressed when I had everything I wanted? I was living the dream! But my depression had never gone away because it doesn't go away. I had been so distracted by the shiny top of the mountain that I hadn't realised I was actually sliding, at quite a speed, towards the bottom of it. Backwards.

It wasn't just during the week that I was drinking. It wasn't all just for work purposes. Entire weekends were written off. I would drink from Friday lunchtime to Sunday evening to quell the fear of the Monday morning label meeting. The meeting involved sitting round a table with the CEO and heads of department, talking about sales and campaigns and watching music videos we had overseen. If the CEO didn't like the video, or if you hadn't sold enough records, he would go for you right there in front of all your peers. Nobody ever stood up for anyone else. Everyone was just pleased that you were the victim and they weren't. Criticism was never professional or constructive, it was personal and vicious. The heads of department, who were mostly middle-class white men, were generally safe. The females and the younger members of staff not so much. They tended to get blamed and often humiliated. The boys had a rapport with the CEO – that rapport being based, as far as I could tell, around the fact they all had penises. The more senior women in the room (and there weren't a lot of them) tended to act like the men to get through those meetings, and some of them their careers. They had a hardness about them. I wasn't sure how to attain this hardness and I wasn't sure if I wanted it. It was horrendous. I cannot imagine any other work environment where treating people like that would be acceptable.

Some of the things I was asked to do during my time in music were, quite literally, unbelievable. I would do anything to be in the inner circle, but in reality, I was always just outside it looking in. If I voiced concern or even an opinion, I was told I was too *something* – too emotional, too bossy, too aggressive, too much – and I was told this by men. I'm not sure the men I worked with were ever described using those words by the men that said those words to me. So that's what I continued to tell myself. I was very, very uncomfortable being in my own skin – except when I was drunk. I wanted the music industry and the people in it to love me, and sometimes they behaved like they did, so I would always go back for more. Always.

There were good times – of course there were. I went to some incredible gigs, hundreds and hundreds of them. I have boxes of tickets and wristbands and passes under my bed that remind me of what a fucking great time it was. I met and hung out with some of my heroes. I once shared a cab with Brandon Flowers. I took Ed Sheeran out for dinner in a terrible pub because nobody else was interested. Dave Grohl gave me a pet name (Goth Girl, thanks for asking), I went to the Brits, I made friends with Michael Eavis by asking him about his cows (this would come in handy later in life). I stood side of stage at Glastonbury, I accidentally got a cab from Reading to London with Keira Knightley, I made epic music videos, won awards and hung out with some incredible people. There is also so much I can't remember. Incredible moments that most people would have cherished for the rest of their lives, just gone from my memory because I was so drunk. And I did have one or two amazing managers. Both of them disappeared, just like my dad did. There one day with promises of promotions and career development, gone the next.

My dream job had made things worse because I'd gone into it with no coping strategy whatsoever. I thought I would become a unicorn, but I was no closer to finding out who the fuck Allie Bailey was. In fact, I was further away because I just couldn't risk being even a tiny bit myself in that environment. I couldn't risk being vulnerable, asking for help, telling the truth. I was so lost. The shame of some of the things I did and put up with while I worked in music still burns; it makes me shudder. The shame of what I was complicit in is there too. There are people I am still in touch with whose lives were destroyed by that industry. Maybe if I'd been braver, or cleverer, or if I'd just known then what I know now, I could have helped them.

I didn't really talk to anyone about how shit I felt. I'd mention it in a funny way now and again, but it actually wasn't that funny. Deep down, I knew the depression was there and it was getting worse all the time. It was like living with an unwelcome but constantly growing lodger. I kept it hidden in a cupboard in my chest. I hid it from everyone because I didn't want people to know it was there or find out the scale of it. I kept it hidden from myself, slamming the door on it when it poked its head out, because I thought if I could get happy it would just go away. From the second year of my career, I was regularly medicating with booze from about lunchtime, which then seeped into a dinner time at which there would be no dinner. At one point, I didn't eat a proper meal for three months, not because I had an eating disorder, but because I was too depressed to eat. I constantly felt sick and scared. I survived on cigarettes, bananas, ice pops, lager and the occasional packet of crisps. I called this the 'Winehouse diet' and thought it was cool.

When I moved out of the flat I'd shared with my future ex-husband, the landlord came to pick up the keys. She looked at me and said brightly, 'How do you stay so slim?' I weakly smiled at her and shrugged. It was the first nice thing anyone had said to me in weeks. What I should have said was, 'borderline manic depression and suicidal thoughts mainly – oh, and the Winehouse diet'. I weighed seven stone. I was twenty-eight. I hadn't seen a doctor since university, and I wasn't planning on seeing one anytime soon. I was a royal fucking mess.

At the end of my marriage, my dad (who I very rarely spoke to) placed me in a flat his partner owned just off Oxford Street, on my own. I was very lucky. Always lucky. Saying that (and I will always be grateful to my dad for saving me from homelessness), there is actually no worse place for a depressed, alcohol-dependent, semi-suicidal twenty-eight-year-old to be than in a flat, alone, in one of the world's greatest drinking cities. Up until this point, I had never, ever lived by myself. I was used to family, housemates, a husband. Now I was completely alone at a time when I needed people more than ever.

I absolutely could not spend time alone with myself sober. At night I would drag people out for drinks after work, or go out by myself and sit in pubs and bars in Soho drinking and staring at the little light on my BlackBerry that meant someone had messaged me. Nobody messaged me. My story went that nobody messaged me because nobody liked me, and nobody wanted to help me. The reality was I never asked for help. The more depressed I got the more paranoid I got. The more paranoid I got, the more I drank to stop the noise in my brain. I thought there was something deeply, deeply wrong with me. I thought I was going to get found out at work as an imposter and that everyone at work was plotting to get rid of me. I thought I was a worthless piece of shit. If I wasn't worthless, why was I alone? I couldn't bear the pain of these thoughts which played on repeat most of the time. I did absolutely nothing to deal with them except attempt to drink them away, which worked for about twenty minutes at a time. It was pretty fucking grim.

Red flags were raised, nobody acted. I remember arranging for my brother to come up from Bournemouth to see me. When he got there, I didn't answer the door because I had been drinking on my own all day and had passed out in bed. Someone smashed the front door in. I still don't know who. My dad and his wife were there. They had been called up from Winchester. My phone had twenty-four missed calls on it. I just sat in the living room stinking of booze while they looked concerned. I don't really remember what happened after that. I think me and my brother went out and got pissed.

Another morning I woke up in bed covered in my own blood. I'd come home that night and fallen into a massive mirror in my bedroom. A slice of the mirror had stuck in my wrist, and I'd obviously gone to the bathroom to take it out. There was blood everywhere. The hallway and bathroom looked like a murder scene, and my bed was soaked in it. I didn't feel well. I cleaned it up as best I could and started my journey to work, but it wouldn't stop bleeding. I bought a big plaster from the chemist, but by the time I got to work, it had soaked through and I had to change it. My boss asked if I was OK. I muttered yes and kept on typing, but blood was dripping on to my keyboard. I was scared. I told my boss I thought I needed to go to hospital, and he called my then boyfriend who worked across the road. He came and got me and took me to the outpatient unit near work where they X-rayed my arms and knees, took the shards of mirror out and stitched me up.

That should have been a wake-up call. It wasn't. There are countless stories like that. This stuff happens to people once or twice in their lives. But it was happening to me all the time. During the week and at weekends. All. The. Time. This had happened throughout my twenties and was still happening now as I approached thirty. I thought about my behaviour – or my perceived inability to control it – a lot. Every time I thought that maybe I should do something about the drinking, that maybe something was wrong, I dismissed it – usually by drinking. The only time I really thought about it, uninterrupted, was when I was running. And I had started running a lot.

CHAPTER 3
RUNNING WON'T SAVE YOU

Listen to: 'Bloodbuzz Ohio' – The National

I started running a few miles here and there towards the end of my marriage. It had been suggested as a way for me to stop feeling so mega shit by the 'slashed my wrists the wrong way' doctor I saw at university. I ignored that advice for years, but one day, after another huge row with my future ex-husband, and feeling like things were going to go one of two ways (throw myself in front of a bus or try to do something else to stop thinking about throwing myself in front of a bus), I ran from my flat in Whitechapel one mile to Tower Bridge and back. I have no idea what prompted that. But those first miles, those first, awful, painful miles run in my Chuck Taylor Converse All Stars and jogging bottoms did something. They stopped the thoughts. They stopped them dead, because I had to think about something else. I had to think about breathing and moving faster than a walk. And when I got back to my flat, I felt fucking amazing. Better than I had felt in months. I had a beer to celebrate.

It's not like suddenly my life changed after that run. The little buzz I got wore off after about twenty minutes. I would go out for a run here and there – literally a couple of miles – but I can't remember it being an epiphany. I didn't love it and I had no running friends, but I did it whenever I felt so wretched that I just wanted to die. And it stopped those feelings for the time I was out. It distracted me. I liked the feeling I got. It felt like a blood transfusion: the bad blood being run out and replaced by good blood; the feelings of terror and depression falling out the bottom of my feet. I got a bike and started riding to and from work some days. That stopped when I was almost killed by a van outside Buckingham Palace. But the little runs continued.

When I started working at the label, a couple of my colleagues were runners, and I felt like one of the lads being able to talk to them about it. One of them had run a marathon, and I was in total awe. I'd lived in London for a while and was very, very aware of 'the Marathon', but I never gave the idea of doing it a second thought. Some of my colleagues suggested we go for the occasional run, and as Hyde Park was just outside our building, I agreed. Going for a run not only kept me out of the pub for at least one lunchtime a week, it also quietened my mind a bit. I found afternoons easier to deal with, and that end-of-the-day pint was so much more deserved if I got some exercise. I liked this idea that I was a runner. It meant I couldn't possibly have a drinking problem. Runners don't have drinking problems.

I did my first 10k race aged twenty-seven because the lunchtime work run squad said we should do it. I wore a hoodie, my trusty Converse and tracksuit bottoms. It was in Staines. I remember physically struggling out of the hoodie about five miles in, while still running along, and dramatically throwing it in a bush. I remember crossing that finish line and thinking, *Fuck me, I did it!* I was given a medal. It was the first medal I had ever been given for anything. A physical embodiment of 'you are enough'. I've still got it somewhere.

I started going out for those lunchtime runs on my own. I'd discovered running could actually semi-cure a hangover while also proving to myself that there was absolutely no drinking or depression problem for at least twenty minutes. I would run around thinking, *I am fine. This is fine. Look at me. I am a runner*. I was running about four miles twice a week and had downloaded the Nike+ app. I liked it when it told me I'd just done my fastest 5k. I was all about fast. I'd started reading running magazines, and fast was definitely the thing to be. *This is good,* I thought. *It makes me feel OK while I am doing it and it stops me being in the pub.* The fact that I could register that not being in the pub was a good thing should have been a warning sign to me. A tiny voice in my head asked, *Why can't you just choose not to go to the pub, Allie? Why do you have to do something else?* I ignored that voice and cracked on with my run. What a ridiculous thing to think. I'd go to the pub after work anyway; I deserved a pint after all this running.

I have absolutely *no* record of my weekly running from the time I started. Maybe I have it in the depths of Strava (I eventually binned off Nike+ when it wouldn't register 100-mile runs as distance), but I do know that I finally signed up to do the London Marathon for charity in 2013, and I do know that I trained for it like a bastard.

It would be lovely to interject here with a bit about how slowly running was saving me, but it wasn't. It was masking a lot. A couple of years before I ran that first marathon, I met someone who I fell desperately in love with, and after an incredible game of chase (by me), he ended up being my boyfriend. In order to snag this person, I'd had to do a lot of pretending, a lot of hiding my acute drinking problem and a lot of being 'the best version of myself'. Being 'the best version of myself' involved doing more running and appearing like I was sorting my shit out. In reality, I was only 'the best version of myself' when I was *actually* running. Running had in no way changed what went on when I *wasn't* running, and so that meant *pretending* I was sorting my shit out when I absolutely was not. I thought if I pretended/acted like the person that the new love of my life wanted me to be, then I would magically become that person. This would definitely work.

I never questioned *anything* about the new love of my life's behaviour towards me, which for the most part was lovely. Occasionally, however, it would veer into the hypercritical and it was sometimes just fucking mean. Any criticism thrown at me incited absolute fear he would leave me, so on the surface I changed the behaviour he didn't like and tried to be what he wanted me to be all the time. This went on for five years. Another slice of my existence where I felt like I would be found out at some point, an imposter in my own life.

Another reason to silence it when it reared its head with a few social drinks.

While I was training for London, I lived like a saint. I stopped drinking and smoking for eighty days. I know it was eighty days because I marked every fucking day off on a calendar, like I was in prison. I was following a *Runner's World* training plan literally by the book, and in all honesty, I did feel better. I was very, very focused on finishing the marathon – some might say distracted by it – and because it was only for a short time, I did manage to stop drinking, because I knew I could start again. I moved in with the new love of my life and I left my job at the label for a new one. New boyfriend, new job, new hobby, new me (for about thirty per cent of the time). Running was playing a part here. It was the only time I had to myself where I could freely think thoughts that I would otherwise bury. The thoughts weren't threatening out on training runs. They floated by, I acknowledged them and I moved on to the next thing. Even in those early days, it was the only time I really felt like me or at least the me that I wanted to be. I liked how I felt like a normal person; normal people go running, depressed alcoholics don't. I liked the pain, I liked battling through it. I liked the weather; I liked it when it rained and was cold and I was the only one out on the roads. And I bloody *loved* it when I finished the London Marathon. I loved the noise, the applause, the crowds, the validation; I loved everything about it.

Something happened inside me when I crossed that finish line. A little spark went off, a little spark that I now recognise as pure, unadulterated enoughness. I was so fucking proud of myself. I cried. I was on TV. My mum was proud of me, my sister was proud of me, everyone was proud of me. I had done something that everyone in the whole world knew was hard. I had another 'you are enough' medal – one that was recognised worldwide as a symbol of excellence. Dopamine levels shot through the roof and external validation rained down on me. And absolutely nothing changed.

The high of the marathon lasted approximately twenty-four hours before I started berating myself for not getting a sub-four finish. That sub-four finish was my aim. I had read about it in the running magazines. Sub-four. Sub-four. Sub-fucking-four. That's what meant you were good. I had come in at 4.03. I was not very good.

The not-good-enough story was back, and it was rioting. It began to overshadow any pride or achievement I'd felt previously. It was fucking loud. The time off the booze had been just as hard as the training and fundraising. I obviously got absolutely shitfaced the minute the whole thing was over and didn't run again for about three months. I was back to exactly the way things should be. How they were before. And to save about 30,000 words, this cycle went on for a few years: train for the London Marathon, go back to where you were. Train for the London Marathon, go back to where you were. Running was not saving me. Running doesn't save anyone. While it may be therapeutic, it is not therapy. It is not a magic bullet. What running was doing was buying me time. It was buying me time for those thoughts about the things I didn't want to think about. Over and over again while out training those thoughts would crop up. *This would be so much easier without a hangover, why don't you feel this calm at home? Do you think XXXX really loves you? Why do you act differently around him? Why are you such an arsehole to yourself? Wouldn't it be nice to not feel like that? Do you think maybe you have a problem with alcohol?* Running allowed me to spend time with these thoughts without distraction. It was almost like I was cheating on my non-running brain with my running brain. Did I act on these thoughts? Rarely, if ever. But I let them be, and the more they cropped up, the more they left an imprint. I just couldn't see a way to feel like this when I wasn't running. So, I started running more and more and more – looking for those calm conversations I just couldn't have in real life.

Event-wise, I was chasing that now-XXL, rose-tinted feeling I had had when first crossing the finish line, and that meant getting faster. In my head, the point of an event was to prove over and over again that you were better than the year before. Success is measured in time with running. That's what I'd read in the magazines. The only question I ever got asked about my running was, 'What's your PB?', so I started to attach a good part of my own self-worth to that number. Nowadays, I cannot think of anything more ridiculous. It started to ruin my training runs, and the time I had to think about things clearly was taken up with other thoughts: the *you're not good enough* ones, the looking-at-your-watch ones. When you think about people asking after your times, it's just fucking weird. What does it *mean*? It's personal and depends on so many different variables, some of which you're in control of and others which you're not. There is literally no planet on which comparing your time with someone else's is helpful, but I did it constantly. I would train hard for the London Marathon five months of the year and trot about doing half-marathons the rest of the time. The only difference now was that I knew I could get away with doing the training *and* the drinking, and sometimes I could mash the two together. Jokes aside, I sometimes think that the endurance I have now is partially down to being utterly fucking hanging for a good part of my running career. Almost every race I ran in my thirties was done with a hangover.

That first marathon is an example of a time I can clearly remember thinking I was totally in control of the drinking. I'd proved it by stopping. During the early days of my first music job and during a couple of periods between labels, I'd stop drinking for a few weeks here and there. These were almost always times where I thought 'things had changed' and I was that person I'd wanted to be. I had a new job, or a new relationship, I was running a race, etc., etc., and I was magically not depressed for a few weeks. I didn't link drinking with depression or depression with drinking. My view was that people, events and things outside of me *made* me depressed. I did not see it as an illness and did not give it the respect that an illness deserves. I thought I could make it go away using shiny new things: jobs, clothes, relationships, running. I never addressed or dealt with it, and I absolutely *never* accepted it. I saw acceptance as a weak thing, a backing-down thing, a thing that means you have given up and have no choice.

When I eventually stopped drinking for good, almost ten years later, it took over a year to get to the point where I understood this. The fact I didn't have this information and was not willing to face up to it meant that I would stay in this depressive cycle for another decade. That's heartbreaking to write, but that's what happened. If you're sitting reading this and see yourself here, please stop and think about what you haven't accepted. Acceptance is not weakness. Acceptance is absolute balls-to-the-wall power. Anyway, I digress.

One thing I did notice about my short bursts of sobriety was that stopping was really hard. When I wasn't drinking, I thought about alcohol *a lot*. Maybe five to ten times a day. I felt angry when I didn't have it or wasn't allowed booze – like I was missing out. I would get agitated and snappy. I couldn't socialise. When I had to socialise, I told *everyone* I was training for a marathon or on Dry January as if not drinking was some sort of massive social faux pas. And the reason I felt like not drinking was a massive social faux pas is because it fucking is. Still.

The possibility that thinking about alcohol this much wasn't normal was starting to register with me more and more often. When the idea that maybe I *did* have a problematic relationship with it came up when I *wasn't* running, I squashed it back down inside me. When it came up when I *was* running, I did listen. For the time I was running. Then I forgot about it. Silly running thoughts.

No, I concluded, I was definitely in control. Definitely. I had to be. There was evidence: managing to stop for eighty days prior to that first marathon; another Dry January. I can take it or leave it really. My choice. I felt like I was growing up a bit anyway and was nowhere near as bad as I used to be. My choice. Take it or leave it. I wanted to take it all the time.

Even when I wasn't drinking 'a lot' (which was rare and usually because I was in polite company or being forced to share wine), I was still *thinking* about drinking a lot. I was always wondering where the next drink would come from. If I could get away with just one more in the pub I would. I'd get ratty when people started leaving after just one drink. I'd worry when the levels in the wine bottle got low. I'd 'accidentally' order a bottle of wine in restaurants instead of a glass, then I would watch like a hawk as people shared it among their glasses and feel angry if someone had more than me. If I was going out to meet people, I would have at least half a bottle before I got there and not tell anyone. When I got back from nights out, I was the first to reach for the nightcap – then, whoops! Where has the time gone? We've drunk the whole bottle LOL.

While cohabiting with the love of my life, I drank 'responsibly' with dinner almost every night, and then would take secret swigs out of the bottle every time I went into the kitchen until that bottle was gone. He didn't drink wine, so he never noticed – or he never said anything if he did. I believed I was in control because I'd proved I could stop if I had to, and I didn't drink in the mornings, and I didn't drink spirits, and I had a nice boyfriend, and I was a runner. Utter delusion with a side salad of squashed-down feelings of knowing that there was something very wrong somewhere. Feelings ignored. Feelings numbed.

The more I ignored these feelings, the worse they got. The more I hid them, the bigger they grew. I could hide how I really felt about myself from everyone but me. Even though I was running longer and longer distances. I was literally running away from having to deal with it. The not-good-enough story that I'd metaphorically shoved in the same cupboard as the depression crept back in. I may well have had a new job, but it was in the same shitty industry. I may well have had a lovely boyfriend, but I lived my life expecting him to find out I was a cunt and abandon me. I may well have been running marathons and now ultramarathons, but I was not dealing with either elephant in the room: the depression or the alcoholism. The cycle restarted like a fucking bush fire.

I kept finding evidence as to why I wasn't enough for my boyfriend, or for my job, or a good enough runner. I found some actual evidence and lots of completely made-up evidence. Very little fact and lots and lots of fiction. Little triggering things that happened at work. Little triggering things that happened at home. My boyfriend didn't like me smoking, my boyfriend had picked up on how much I was drinking and how often and he hated it, my boyfriend didn't like my tattoos, so I went and got more and lied to him about it. My boyfriend didn't want to get married. I started to turn the screws. It was happening.

I asked him outright if he would ever marry me. He said he didn't believe in marriage. He asked me if I'd ever have kids. I told him I didn't want to pass on my mental health issues. Stalemate. I suggested we meet halfway and get married *and* have a baby. I would have a baby if he would marry me, because I fucking loved him. He said no. He said he would never marry anyone. I heard I was not enough for him to marry and have a baby with. I went into spin cycle. I convinced myself I had been proved right. Not enough. Piece of shit. *He's found out you're not what you say you are.* Not worthy. The pressure of the trauma and anger and rage and hurt and depression and drinking made me feel like my skin was too tight for my body. And so what did I do about it?

I did nothing. I let it all happen. I let it all come crashing down around me in exactly the same way it had done before. *I'll show you I'm not enough, first love of my life. Hold my beer while I show you just how awful I can be.* I cheated on him while I was off my face with a bloke who was in a band I was working with. He was utterly heartbroken. And I was numb. I had ruined what could have been the greatest romantic relationship of my life. I had pressed self-destruct again and really, really hurt someone I loved very, very much because I couldn't believe that he loved me. And now this person who I had loved and who, in hindsight, had helped steer me closer to the straight and narrow absolutely fucking hated me.

We did split up. And I had to move out. I tried to get back together with him loads of times: dramatic drunken scenes at weddings where I begged him, me shouting at him at gigs. *That's the way to do it, Allie! You show him what he's missing!* It was a shitshow.

Many years later, he would go on to meet someone, marry them and have a baby. I want to use this opportunity to tell him that I am really, really sorry for behaving like I did. He didn't deserve it.

Fast forward six years. It's 2017 and I have just published that blog right back at the start of this section; it was written six years *after* the first time I thought I was turning things around. Six years after I split up with the first love of my life. Six years in which I changed jobs twice but didn't really change jobs at all. It was written nine years after I started running. Not running a bit. Running a lot. By 2017, I had completed forty marathons and seventeen ultras. I was properly running. Yet still I wrote a blog about wanting to die. You may well be sitting there going, 'Hang on, Bailey, I thought this was about how running changed your life? I thought there was no wall? This looks a lot like a fucking wall to me.' We'll get to that bit, I promise we will.

That blog makes me seriously worried about my next steps – and I know what my next steps were. Reading it back is almost like watching a movie with two possible endings and hoping to God it's the happy one. It wasn't the one it should have been. That would make this a very short book. That breakdown was fucking serious. It should have been enough, but it wasn't. I was out-of-control ill, and very few people knew about it then, or now.

When I got back to London in October 2017 after taking a ridiculously short week to 'get better', I continued with my life as best I could, feeling wretched. I continued my life as I had done for the previous twenty years. I stopped, breathed and continued. I hoped 'it' would go away. I hoped the depression would go away. I hoped that was my rock bottom over and done with. Wasn't that bad, was it? And I had a 100-miler to run. I was convinced that would be the making of me. I was convinced that would change me. For information, running a 100-mile race is not and never has been a successful way of dealing with depression or addiction. It has never been recommended to anyone by any medical professional ever, mainly because it's fucking stupid and doesn't work.

By 2017, I was reliant on alcohol mentally and physically. I had been for years. I knew this, I just didn't accept it. I dismissed any idea I might have about myself being an alcoholic by telling myself all the usual stories. I was functioning. I was a runner. I could not, however, envisage a life without drinking. If *anyone* dared to tell me they thought that I had a problem (and believe me people did), I usually told them to fuck right off. I was fit and healthy; I was an ultrarunner with depression who liked a drink – just like everyone else does. It wasn't the drink making me depressed, I just was depressed, OK? If anything, it was the depression making me drink. I was who I was. I was broken inside. I was just fucking broken. That's how it was. That was how it would be forever. I would run 100 miles to prove everyone wrong. Watch me. I would get very, very angry when people gently asked if I thought I had a problem. So they stopped asking.

I went into the race just a week or so after returning to London post-breakdown. I was fixated on the idea that running 100 miles would somehow fix me for good. How could it not? I really was grasping at straws now. The night before the event I drank the best part of two bottles of red wine, socially, with a couple of mates over dinner. I tried to have sex with someone I barely knew. I went to bed late. I was scared, anxious, depressed, nervous. Running 100 miles would fix me. Autumn 100 – here we go.

I'd love to write a paragraph here about how it *did* fix me, but it didn't. In a lot of ways at that point in my life it made things worse. It was fucking tough. It was always going to be, but on a hangover it was a teeny bit more tough than it should have been. I had so much support from people: from the marshals I knew on course to my friends and family who came to see me on the route – the first and last time a lot of them did that. I quickly fell into a sort of weird ultra-trance, and while I can remember bits of it vividly, there's a lot I can't. The highlights are the kindness I was shown from other competitors, the Centurion staff and my pacers. Despite being a mess, I ran and paced really well, coming in at just under twenty-four hours. It was uneventful for the most part – it was wet, windy and dark in more ways than one – but the lasting memory comes from the last six miles as I struggled along the Thames, hoping to get that longed-for sub-twenty-four-hour time. About six miles from the end, I started to cry. At the time I put this down to pain, fatigue, pride, relief. I now think it was something different. I think it was the realisation that this event had not changed me. The realisation I was the same. The fact I'd put my eggs in the magic 100-mile basket and they'd all broken. I was running out of options here. Why didn't I feel any different?

This was all reflected in the post-race blog I wrote and posted at the time. Reading it back I just think, *What a load of bollocks*. It was like I was trying to convince myself that something had changed. That blog contains the following paragraph:

> When I came into the hall [at the end of the race] and saw my mum, when my sister ran down the last part of the path to meet me, the demon was beaten, 100 miles. 23 hours 35 mins. The demon was beaten.

No it fucking wasn't. I hadn't beaten anything. I had *wanted* to beat it, I had *wanted* to leave it all out there. But had I? Fuck no! I was refusing to accept my situation and dressing it up in the way I wanted it to be. People do that all the time. It's called motivated reasoning. In the last six miles, cracks had appeared in my own internal narrative: *You are the same person, you feel no different, just a bit more tired. This hasn't worked. This isn't going to change you.*

And that's what I mean when I talk about running buying me time. From the twenty-three hours and thirty-five minutes that I was out there, that was the one thought worth listening to, but it was the one I chose to ignore because it wasn't in keeping with my own beliefs about what a 100-mile race could do for me, or more importantly what I *wanted* it to do for me. It would be another week until I acknowledged that it hadn't worked.

BLOG EXCERPT: PUBLISHED 28 OCTOBER 2017, ONE WEEK AFTER THE AUTUMN 100

> I really thought I was making steps to push forward, that I had left a small part of this horror somewhere on the Ridgeway in Goring. But no. Just like that, on a train home from seeing my brothers and sister for an evening of drinks and laughing, it smacks me in the face like a long-lost fucking cousin. I self-medicate, as well as NHS-medicate, with alcohol. I feel awkward socially and so I mask it with booze. I did that last night. It's coming. I feel a tremor of panic when my sister drops me in the village to get the train back to London. I go to a nearby pub and sit there to wait for the train. I drink beer. When I order the beer, I

sound normal and confident. I am terrified of myself. I look at Facebook. Engagements. Babies. Impending doom. I get on the train. The train takes two hours and there is no buffet car and I feel wretched, and to be honest I have lost those two hours, but I wasn't asleep. That fucking doom. Everything black. I start thinking about what a terrible person I actually am. How I present myself as a bastion for love and trust and open communication, but how I have let people down, cheated on people and ruined the things I have loved. What's the fucking point? Is this a suicidal thought? Was that? Is this? Is thinking about suicidal thoughts actually suicidal thoughts, or is it just thinking about them? What's the fucking point? When will I be better? How fast do the trains go through this station? Would that kill me? Sometimes I wonder if I actually want to be better or if this is so much a part of me that I am not willing to let it go. Is this actually a comfort? Why is being a person so fucking complex and fraught with pain? I do want to be better. I want to be glorious, but I don't know how.

Back to square one.

PART TWO
THE RECKONINGS

Just before we delve head first into this, let's have a recap. I thought it would be OK to run my first 100-mile race just a few days after having one of the worst mental health crises of my adult life. I then thought that just a couple of weeks after that it would be OK to head to one of the booziest capital cities in the world with one of my best friends and unaware enablers to see a band that make me cry on my best days and make me want to die on my worst. What could possibly go wrong? At the time, I had been on a new batch of antidepressants, Citalopram, for around three weeks.

BLOG EXCERPT: DOWN AND DOWN IN PARIS (AND LONDON)

Published 5 November 2017
Age: 36
Years drinking: 22
Years running: 9
Listen to: 'Pink Rabbits' – The National

It's 5 November 2017 and I am sitting in a beautiful hotel room in Paris unable to go outside, unable to stop crying. I try to eat breakfast, but every swallow feels like the hardest thing I have ever done, and even drinking water is difficult. Basic human needs are a huge problem again.

I have been in Paris with Cat (my best friend and housemate) for four days. We came to see The National – a band we love – and we decided to stay on for a few days to hang out with friends and spend some time together. Cat has been there through this whole thing with me, not just this time around, but for many years before. Today I was supposed to go with her to hang out with an old friend and his children, but last night we went out and got in at 3 a.m. Yesterday I tried to prepare myself; I tried to eat properly and drink enough water and get ready to spend time with people. I controlled my wine intake. I still drank wine. I saw friends during the day, had lunch, walked around Paris. I felt OK. Not great but OK. We stayed out late talking with another friend. We drank more wine. We were happily drunk. I've not been sleeping well on this trip.

This morning I feel like I did that day at Tottenham Court Road: completely detached from reality. Horror, fear, paranoia, fits of tears, hopelessness. I tell her I can't go out. I can't be around people, and I can't be around children. I can't stop crying, and I keep thinking if this is all there is then what's the point in living? I am back to square one in a beautiful hotel in Paris. I have let her and them down. I can't even fulfil the most basic of responsibilities. She takes me downstairs for coffee, and we talk it through, and she asks things like have I been taking my drugs? (I missed one yesterday.) Is it because we have been drinking too much this week? (More of that later.) I try to explain, yes and no, it is all and none of these things. It is a life I am currently confined to. I go out with her to buy bread for the friend she is visiting. That floating feeling I get when I am walking returns. I feel panicky and lost. I put her in an Uber and go back to the hotel, and that is where you find me now.

I'm going to do something now that I have not done before in a public forum. I'm going to talk about the other demon that is best friends with the one that lives inside my brain (depression) but is more physical. That one's name is alcohol. I have used it most days since I was fifteen. I have used it to party. I have used it to try to drown the depression. I can make the depression black out if I drink enough of it, but the next day he is there and he's worse because he's been fed. So I use it again to quieten him. And on it goes. And on it goes. And on it goes. And there have been times when I have almost convinced myself that I am a complete alcoholic. But I don't drink in the morning, so that must mean I'm not. And I have a job and a home, and I am functioning, so that must mean I'm not. And I can go a day or two without it, so that means that I'm not. And I can go out and just have one pint (but most of the time it's three or four), so that means I'm not. And I don't want to be an alcoholic, so that must mean I'm not. My job demands it. My social life demands it. All my friends do it and ask me to come and do it with them. These things and people demand it. I feel like I have no choice. I know other people who suffer like me, and when we go out, we go out and drink because that's what we do, and it helps us to open up and we talk about depression and drink because that's what we do. It builds up and up, over weeks of going out and being social and trying to manage my illness until I don't eat any more because I feel awful and I am not hungry, and I shake and I can't concentrate and that's when the other monster is at his best. And I have proved what a complete prick I am by not being able to control something as simple as my own drinking habit. And I feel awful, so I drink some more.

I drink on my own and with people. More with people than on my own, but I still drink on my own very regularly. I think it's empowering for me to be able to go and sit and have a glass of wine alone. In reality, it's actually not. It's fucking stupid.

I question why I drink to try to rationalise it. Does it make me feel good? Yeah, for a while. Does it make me more interesting? Yeah, and more confident and that's how I can go and be glorious in front of people. Does it relax me? Yeah, it does. Is it ruling and ruining my life? Yes, it most definitely is. Can I stop drinking? I don't honestly know. Am I killing myself with it? Yes, I am. Is this going to fuck up my dreams of changing my career? Will it ruin my running? Yes, it will. I haven't run for two weeks. I've been tired from the 100-miler, my legs are sore, but I have also been hungover and miserable every fucking day. I have been hungover for the majority of my twenties and thirties.

I am red wine party girl. I am red wine, get drunk, be darkly hilarious party girl, and if you're a man, stay the fuck away from me because I will destroy you. But I have always taken it too far. I am a blackout drunk. Not all the time, but I am capable of it some of the time. If I am going to be completely honest, my alcohol intake has played a direct part in the destruction of every important romantic relationship I have ever had. A tiny part of me is wondering if I am drinking too much, but the depression silences that – nah, you're fine. Just a couple. And depression comes and goes and comes and goes and comes and goes. The one thing I have never changed? I have never stopped drinking. And when my depression is at its worst, what do you do? You drink. And when you drink, the silence only comes for an hour or so and then the pain, the fractured sleep, the hangover, the depression, and so what is the fucking point of drinking? I don't want to never drink again. That frightens me. I want to drink normally. But I don't know how to do that. And that means for now, I have to stop. Just for today. I have to stop. An adult lifetime addiction that, for now, has to stop.

After I wrote this, I published it on a hidden blog so nobody could read it. I hid my shame in a corner of the internet. And I kept drinking.

CHAPTER 4
WELL, THAT ESCALATED QUICKLY

Listen to: 'Backroads' – Lonely the Brave

Between 2013 and 2018, I ran seventy-one marathons or ultramarathons. Seventy-fucking-one. These events ranged from trail marathons to multi-day epics in the UK and beyond. I was drinking the entire time.

I never, ever hit The Wall during a race. Ever. I never didn't finish either; my first DNF (Did Not Finish) would come a good six months into my sobriety. At the time, I thought that made me fucking amazing at running. I didn't find running easy; running is hard, and ultras are hard. I felt pain, I got injured, wet, cold, hungry, tired, I threw up, I shat myself and I cried a lot. I scraped the barrel in some of those events, but for me, in running there was no wall. I always got the job done.

My day-to-day life was a totally different ball game. There was a wall. In fact, there were a number of them. Walls that I had built but was, at this point, completely unaware and totally accepting of. I didn't even give them the name 'wall'. The fact I could go out and smash up a 100-mile coastal route over three days without thinking about the possibility of a wall, all while living inside the confines of one I had created in my own head, is pretty insane. This extreme contradiction in my own make-up is absolutely fascinating to me.

How could I maintain this belief I was not good enough in most aspects of my life, but be so focused and gutsy when it came to running? How could I behave like a prisoner in my own head, believing I had no option but to self-medicate and stay anchored in misery, but be so hell-fucking-bent on getting the job done in an event?

I've come up with loads of reasons for this. Maybe it's because running is tangible. Running has a start, a middle and an end. You have very clear instructions on what is expected, and it is a solo endeavour. Nobody else can do the running for you. Nobody else can affect the outcome. There are a number of certainties attached to it: the distance, the terrain, the amount of training you have to do. Running does not judge or discriminate; it is a leveller. If you want to run a marathon and not die, you have to do the work. It's a very clean process. It's very clear. It's very honest. It's very simple. When you complete the task that is set, you usually get given a medal – proof that you have completed the task to a high enough standard to be given a reward. And that feeling you get when that medal goes round your neck? That is the feeling of being enough, even if only for two minutes. Maybe that was the high I was chasing. Maybe that is why I didn't think there was a wall, why I did so many races. Or maybe it was to prove to everyone that I wasn't an alcoholic. Or because it totally took me out of my own life for a few hours. Or it was a brutal attempt at self-harm. Or maybe, just maybe, I was in search of that peace.

Running became a break from myself. It was only at the start of runs that I doubted myself; it was only then that the negative voices bothered me. I would tell them to fuck off; sometimes I would actually shout, 'Just FUCK OFF', at them. And they went. It was like my brain was an annoying child on a long car journey asking if we were nearly there yet. If I threw some hills and technical trail at them, they would be distracted and shut up. So that's what I did. And that's why the races got longer, harder and more technical. The big road races became increasingly difficult. My brain loved those because there was evidence of how shit I was everywhere in the form of thousands of other people performing better than me. If the voices did get too much, I would just have a drink and crack on. Sometimes I drank before races, sometimes I drank during them. I started the 2015 London Marathon on the back of three hours' sleep with the world's worst hangover. Breakfast was a croissant, a Mayfair Blue and half a pint of warm white wine. I came in at 3.54. My marathon PB of 3.36 came at the end of a three-day bender in Berlin. I don't remember much about that race except thinking, *Fuck, I've gone out too fast*, at mile fourteen and being disappointed that the beer at the end was alcohol-free. Running wasn't saving me. It was kind of enabling me.

When I first started on the ultras and long trail runs, I was using the events and training like I used alcohol: as a numbing agent. Long, demanding and technical races meant I couldn't think about how much I hated myself because there were other things to do – like not die. This shit was hard, and I needed to concentrate. When I started, I was doing something that theoretically was really good for me as a distraction from the never-ending shitshow that was my mental health and lifestyle. As time went on and those distances became more manageable (because I'd done loads of them), I began to have more time to myself in my head. Time to get to know myself a bit better. Time to think a bit more clearly about things: situations, problems, worries. Like all thoughts, they were fleeting – some of them helpful, some of them not. But I'd also have other thoughts. Weird ones. Thoughts like, *Wow, it's a beautiful day, what an incredible view, I could just do this forever.* Positive thoughts that I allowed to linger in my brain instead of dismissing as bullshit.

Most of these ultras and trail marathons were outside London, and every time I got on the train home, I felt deflated and scared. Not sometimes, every time. The routine was the same. I drank the train wine, got the Tube, went to the pub on my own with my medal, took a photo for Instagram, went home, drank some more wine and usually passed out. Then I would book another race as soon as possible. I wanted to feel the way I did when I was running all the time, but I didn't think it was possible to do that without actually running.

In December 2017, I got a message from someone I sort of knew that read, 'Do you want to come on an adventure?' Being desperate to be anywhere but where I was, I replied, 'Sure, as long as it's not cold.' Fast forward to January 2018, and I touched down at Ulaanbaatar airport. It was -40 °C and I was about to attempt to run 100 miles across the largest frozen lake in Mongolia. Nobody had ever done this before. It was a world first.

I was essentially a guinea pig sent as part of a small team to test the route, the accommodation, etc., to see if it could work as a public event and to see if anyone would die doing it. I was up for anything that would get me out of the UK and out of my own brain. This was another example of a time where I thought, *If I can do this, I'll be fixed.*

Mongolia was insane. It was like being in a very old, cold film. Being with that group was exactly like being on the trails. I felt accepted, welcomed and part of a team. I had a tangible job to do, to get across this lake and not die. So that is what I would do. I felt like an adventurer, an explorer, a trailblazer. I felt like I mattered. It was an incredible opportunity, and it took me out of my little London prison and out of my little brain prison and plonked me in a place that I had rarely if ever been to – the place where you have to face yourself with no distraction and no escape. Some people call that place 'the moment'.

That trip was fucking hard work, not least because of the environment we were thrown into. Staying warm/alive was the number one priority. Then there was the small matter of twenty-five miles a day for four days straight. I had begged and borrowed kit to keep warm, but when it came to the running part, none of us really knew what we were doing; it was all trial and error. The nights spent camping out on the islands that rose up from the middle of the lake were terrifying. One night, temperatures dropped to -45 °C, and while I was rolled up in a million jackets, sleeping bags and animal skins, I had moments where I didn't know if I would wake up the next day. It was so cold that ice would develop on the boys' beards as they slept. My eyes stuck together every time they watered. What the fuck was I doing here? I'll tell you what I was doing. I was starting an episode of my life that was more important than I could have ever imagined.

I had some proper moments on that ice. It was my first experience of being in an extreme environment. It strips you down to the bare bones of who you actually are, and I had similar experiences on later trips in Namibia and Panama. There were no distractions here. No mobile phones, texts, internet or mates to call. There was also no judgement of if we were doing well or badly – because nobody had ever done it before. There was just the moment followed by another moment and then another one. All we had to do was not freeze and move forward. Although we were a group, and often travelled within sight of each other on the ice, I spent the majority of my time alone. When my phone allowed, I'd listen to music, but it would eventually get too cold and switch itself off, then one night my headphones froze and snapped in half – and when that happened I only had the silence. And that lake was, for the most part, totally silent.

I don't think people ever actually sit in total silence any more. It's not easy, but I had no other choice. The only sounds were my own breath and the ice occasionally cracking under my feet. It would be like this for ten hours or more, eight of which I would be alone, so there was literally no escape from the thoughts. I had to listen to those thoughts – the good, the bad and the really fucking bad – whether I liked it or not. It was not peaceful in the same way that my big trail runs back home had been. It was uncomfortable. It was difficult. It was unfamiliar. I had no option; I had to feel those feelings. And so I did. I leaned into the pain and discomfort of what I was actually thinking for a few hours a day. And I didn't like what I found.

Sometimes I would cry as I was running. The tears would freeze in my eyes and it hurt so I tried to stop doing that. It was part of the process; it was part of me being me. Looking back, although I absolutely loved Mongolia with all my heart – the silence, the enormity of it, the fear factor and the way of life – the lasting memory I have writing this is the discomfort I felt in my head. I can't even tell you what I was thinking – apparently a common trauma response is to block this stuff out – but I remember feeling desperate and scared of myself. I remember thinking I wouldn't be able to finish it, or that I would let everyone down. I remember feeling like I was trying to tell myself something, but I didn't know what. I felt like my brain was saying, *Allie, listen.* Listen to what? What am I listening to? That sounds fucking mental, but that's how it was. The hours alone would end because there was always an end to the day, and then it would be all big fires and camaraderie and I'd forget that I'd been scared of my own thoughts out on the ice, and I wouldn't tell anyone and we'd all drink semi-frozen beers and have a laugh. On the final night we were invited to the Mongolia Consulate, and I got so fucked up that I can't remember going to bed and almost missed the flight home.

I was now the first woman on earth to have run the entire length of the lake *on* the fucking lake. My first world first. Validation. I had been good enough. Even while thinking I wasn't good enough, I was; that is the nature of time. I didn't understand this back then. I do now. You spend so long thinking you can't do something while you're actually doing it that it's insane. It happens in most ultramarathons. Think about it. You're literally proving yourself wrong step by step.

The Mongolia trip had proved to me that my thoughts alone could not kill me. My thoughts alone couldn't do anything to me. It was how I reacted to them that mattered. On that trip, I had allowed them to be there until I reached other people. I had just allowed them. I had cried, I had tried to understand, but I had not dismissed or distracted myself or drowned them out and it had been OK – but at the time I didn't consciously register this at all.

The minute I was back in Ulaanbaatar I was on the party bus; I didn't want to think about going home (if I had, then maybe that would have served me better), I didn't want to think about how much I hated my life back in London (if I had, then maybe that would have served me better), so I went straight back to what I knew. Although on some level I think I knew there was another way to handle those thoughts, I didn't want to. I was better off being drunk, fun Allie. Getting fucked up was a complete relief after a week of having to listen to myself.

After the type-2 fun of Mongolia, I was invited to take part in a couple more 'test' events: one in Namibia and one in Panama. I was absolutely overjoyed that I had been asked back. Of course, my return to the UK post-Mongolia had been a textbook return to form – back to the usual. Work, drinking, self-hatred and utter despair peppered with some good stuff going on – almost all of which involved running.

Mongolia had definitely had some effects on me that I was registering. I didn't want to do my job any more; I hated it. I wanted the freedom to be able to do more of the adventure stuff. So I started my own marketing business. I managed to procure a boyfriend (not in Mongolia, that would have been mad). There had been a lot of interest in the Mongolia crossing and I'd been on a few podcasts, in the papers and on TV. I was building a bit of a name for myself as someone that ran really far and was OK at it. I won't lie, I fucking loved the attention. I also won't lie and will tell you that before that Lorraine Kelly interview, I had a glass of wine at 7.30 in the morning. Swings and roundabouts. People thought I was something I definitely wasn't, and I knew that, but by now I was the master pretender. While I was more than vocal about my mental health issues during the interviews I did, I absolutely didn't mention the fact I was half-cut during most of them.

Namibia and Panama were two monster projects that were planned to take place in late 2018. I would take a three-week break from work and travel first to South Africa to run 135 miles across the Namibian desert and then fly to Panama to attempt to cross the entire country unsupported on foot via the jungle. It was quite the ask, and my life was less than organised. In fact, it was a fucking mess.

I very, very nearly didn't go on the Namibia and Panama trips. About a week before the Namibia trip, my biggest and most lucrative client unceremoniously fired me. I lost the bulk of my business's income overnight and was terrified that I was going to go bankrupt and would come back and have to move in with my mum. My four-month-old rescue dog, Pickle, was in desperate need of full rehabilitation and couldn't really leave the house. In hindsight, I was also in need of full rehabilitation and shouldn't really have left the house. I couldn't afford the kit for the trip so had crowdfunded the whole thing. I could still afford wine, though.

It was actually my sister who pushed me to go. She paid for my flights, and for that I will be forever grateful. My life in the UK was once again very quickly spiralling out of control and I had made some quite odd decisions (dog, anyone?). My business was failing, my mental health was failing, my finances were failing. I was attempting to solve all of this by heading to the pub every night and fantasising about moving in with my new boyfriend in Somerset but not actually doing anything about it. By the time the trip rolled around I had got into such a state about it that I was no longer looking after myself at all. On the day I was due to fly, I realised I hadn't eaten a proper meal for about three days. With two hours before the cab turned up to take me to the airport, I decided to go to the supermarket to get a sandwich. So I did. And locked my keys, passport and all my luggage in my flat. That's how much of a fucking mess I was.

By all accounts I shouldn't have gone on this trip. But I did go. Something made me go. The door to the rest of my life had been left ajar by Mongolia – and the Namibia and Panama trips ripped that door clean off its hinges.

Attempting to do two massive trips in the space of two and a half weeks was a stupid idea; it would absolutely fuck me physically for a start. Namibia was first up. The aim was to cross the Namib-Naukluft National Park from the gates at the east of the country to the wreck of the *Eduard Bohlen* on the coast to the west. A 135-mile journey across the oldest desert on earth, on foot, over four and a half days. Facing us would be some of the biggest sand dunes in the world, river valleys boasting a whole host of creatures including ostriches, oryx, big cats and black mamba snakes, and nights in a freezing desert, in a tent surrounded by scorpions and hyenas. Glorious stuff. To our knowledge nobody had ever attempted this before. I had no experience of desert running, nobody to ask about it and literally didn't know what I was doing. It was hands down one of the greatest experiences of my life.

When the plane door shut, so did the door to all my problems. I literally didn't think about the shitshow I had left behind in the UK any more. I guess that is why people run away. Once again, I had a job to do, and I was going to get it done. I knew I could do it. Or I thought I knew I could do it, as long as I could cope with the thoughts.

I absolutely loved every second of that trip. From the awe-inspiring miles and miles of sand to the majesty and monstrosity of the dunes to the stillness of the desert at night; a billion stars above us and a moon bigger than any I have seen before or since; this was living. I felt childlike in my wonder at it all. I just felt like a new person. The desert will do that to you. You are physically so far away from anyone else, so far away from the life that you live day to day, that it is completely possible to be a new, clean person. I go back to the desert in my head all the time. I don't have the words to communicate here just how beautiful it is. Depression doesn't exist in the desert. Nothing does, except you as a blank canvas who can achieve anything. It's just a magical place. You want perspective on how much all the shit we worry about matters? Go to the desert.

The event itself was super hard. The days were long and extremely hot, and the terrain was nuts. But every day was different. There are as many different types of sand as there are types of ice: gravel, hard-packed, soft, muddy, duney, salty. You'd be surprised. There's a lot to deal with admin wise: looking after yourself and making sure you're hydrated and fed even when you don't feel like it. Feet. Fucking feet. But I was happy there. Properly happy. The thoughts didn't bother me anywhere near as much as they had in Mongolia, and I think that was because I was protected by the company. We saw people a lot more often; there were lunches under canvas and banter in the evenings. We could hang out and chat, way more than we could in Mongolia because there wasn't the language barrier or the threat of freezing to death. While we had some social time on the ice, it was always short-lived. In Namibia, we would stay up until the early hours talking absolute shit and sharing what little beer we had. It was magical. I loved the company and the chat. Nobody knew what a mess I was, they just saw me as someone that was good at running far. I didn't feel judged. I felt accepted.

The days were intense, covering upwards of twenty-five miles and God knows how many feet of ascent in 40 °C sun, followed by these amazing meals under the stars – nothing to do other than run and sleep. Run and sleep, run and sleep – I loved it. Taking my shoes off and putting my toes in the sand and thinking how amazing that these were the only human feet ever to have touched those particular grains. Incredible. On the last day the run was short – only thirteen miles – and I cried and cried. I didn't want it to end. I never wanted it to end. I didn't want to go back into my head. I didn't want to go back into my life, I just wanted to do this forever. World first number two done: the first female to run across the Namib-Naukluft National Park. Tick.

We still had our little visit to Panama to go, but first a sea-to-summit run up Cape Town's three peaks, Table Mountain, Lion's Head and Signal Hill. There was talk of this being a little add-on to the trip, so we needed to see if it could be done. Off the back of 135 miles in a desert and just fourteen hours before a flight back to the UK to change kit and get another flight to Panama, sure, why not? Because it's fucking stupid is why not. It nearly killed me.

The route was only nine miles long, with about 7,000 feet of ascent, but it took me almost six hours. I got it done, got the little cart thing back down and got back to the airport in time for the flight. I completed this on a red wine hangover that I had cleverly instigated the night before. I still don't really know how I managed that. But I did. I did things very hungover all the time. It was normal.

Panama was then, and is now, one of the hardest things I have ever done. It is also up there with the most important. Panama was what really got me to come face to face with myself. Mongolia and Namibia, while pretty brutal in their nature, had been relatively social affairs when we weren't running: nights around campfires and hanging out with the rest of the crew, decent food and semi-decent rest periods. Both Mongolia and Namibia were also really well supported; we had a crew with us the whole time and we did have the option to stop and get in or on some sort of vehicle if we needed to. Although I felt very alone at times, there was an element of control to those trips, and there was camaraderie and a well thought-out plan. In Panama, there would be none of these things. This was going to be very fucking different.

The aim with Panama was to cross the country on foot, from the

Atlantic coast to the Pacific coast, via the jungle. There was also some packrafting thrown in at the end – twenty-five miles to get to the sea, where we would be rewarded with a boat ride to Bocas del Toro and a night in a super-luxury hotel in the Caribbean. That was what I was holding out for. That island. That was my reward for three weeks' hard graft. That was my carrot on a stick.

The trip was planned to take around seven days, cover around 100 miles and take in almost 20,000 feet of ascent. I was pretty terrified. I had never been to the jungle, but 100 miles seemed pretty manageable, especially as fifty miles of it was road running over the first two days. I'd run 100 miles in under twenty-four hours. I couldn't see this being a problem.

This trip was a seminal time for me. It stretched me beyond the limits of anything I had done before, or anything I have done since, and it took me to some of the worst places I have ever been in my head, sober or otherwise. There's an incredibly detailed blog about it on my website, and I've tried to summarise how that trip affected me here, but I don't know how successful it will be, so bear with.

Panama was in many ways the proper reckoning. It was the reckoning with myself. It was the mirror I needed to hold up so desperately. It was the single greatest learning experience of my life and would go on to shape my recovery, albeit over a period of years. If Mongolia was parkrun, and Namibia was a marathon, Panama was a multi-day epic with one hand tied behind your back. In hell.

The first thing we did was attempt to cross Panama on foot in one day, just because we could. We had time to do that. We were attempting to do it in under twenty-four hours. Due to lost baggage and waiting around at airports there was no downtime. I was thrown straight into it off the back of a three-hour hungover sleep.

The plan was to start at the Atlantic Ocean, near Colón, and run six miles to the Gatun Lake, a major part of the Panama Canal, jump in a kayak, paddle nine miles to the edge of the jungle, get out and run/hike/hack 'thirteen miles' through jungle, along the Panama Pipeline, until we popped out at Gamboa. Then all we had to do was run thirteen road miles to the end of the pipeline and there you go. Done. So, all in, about forty-one miles-ish in a day, crossing a country.

That is what was supposed to happen. Here is what actually happened.

We reluctantly got up at 4.45 a.m. to start the first six-mile run. It was dark and hot and humid, and we were all already very tired and hungry. I was hungover. Breakfast was a yoghurt and a tiny muffin bought from the shop the day before. Perfect.

As the only female on the trip, I felt like I was under quite a lot of pressure. I let the boys get on with it and run ahead, and after six vomit-inducing miles of hot, humid road we got to the edge of the lake where the kayaks were waiting. We partnered up and got in. Let's fucking paddle.

The lake was beautiful. It was serene, stunning and calm. It had crocodiles in it. After nine miles' paddling, we pulled up to the shore and changed from our running shoes into our jungle boots and kit. The air was so thick I felt like I couldn't breathe. A huge crocodile whacked its tail out of the water and swam off. Fuck's sake. He was the second one we had seen, the other floating like a murderous log in the middle of the lake before disappearing under the water. I was weirdly not scared. I was too tired and hungover to be scared. The second I set foot in the jungle, I knew it was going to be really fucking hard. The damp, deep leaf litter gave way under our boots. The trees were covered with insects, and there was no discernible path. We had a local guy with us who had 'run this route before'. Not, it turned out, very recently. Within thirty minutes we all silently acknowledged that this was going to be a very long day. This, it turns out, was not even the 'proper' jungle.

It's very hard to explain what it's like in the jungle to people who haven't been there. It's hellish. Everything including your feet is wet from the outset. The air is wet. There is mud – a lot of it. The jungle is not flat, it goes up and down all the time – the downs being very, very difficult to manage. You slip and slide, and there is nothing to hold on to. All the trees are covered in either insects or long, sometimes poisonous, spikes so you can't grab them for balance. We fell over a lot. The swamp-like rivers are passable via bridges – high bridges that are often rotten or 'partially fucked' for want of a better phrase. You have to guess where to put your feet to avoid going through them. We had big packs on, filled with litres of water and food. In my head, thirteen miles was nothing. In the jungle, it may as well have been 130. While your body is moving very slowly, your head is doing 100 miles an hour.

We were attempting to follow the pipeline, but finding it was difficult. To avoid dehydrating, we had to keep stopping to filter water which took time and meant we were getting through our food rations way too fast. I was taking salt tabs every hour, but still felt totally drained. We kept having to stop and check the route. We didn't seem to be getting anywhere. Hacking through, up and over the dense vegetation was a gamble: fallen tree trunks would either hold, or you would fall through rotten bark and be covered in ants and termites, sometimes up to your waist in insects. At one point, we were all so hot we made our way down to a river and just got in it fully clothed. Leeches were mentioned. We all ignored this information. It was almost too hot to function. A few minutes floating in the river gave us a second wind. For about five minutes.

We trekked on and on, soaked in sweat, the realisation dawning that this was not a thirteen-mile section. It was a lot longer than that. We had started to run out of food; there was no way crew could get in to help us. We had someone meeting us on the other side of the jungle with the van. And the food was in the van. I started to worry about the second traverse. The proper traverse. How could anyone survive in here for more than a few hours? How would we survive for four days? Panic had started rising. I was not good enough to do this. I couldn't cope.

It started to get dark. My watch ran out of battery. I didn't know how far I had come, or how far we had left to go. Nobody did. GPS doesn't work brilliantly under a thick canopy. The bats and monkeys started making noises and moving about. I could hear them but not see them. My mind started to go, and I started to hallucinate big black cats and things flying at my face. After what seemed like an eternity, we hit a runnable track and came to a clearing. This was where the van was supposed to be. But it wasn't there.

The crew had left a pile of snacks and drinks – but no van. Where the fuck was the van? We waited. We brushed the ants off the food and ate what we could. We still had a thirteen-mile road section to go in order to complete the crossing, and the boys were talking about whether they could actually go on. It was all I could think about too. I could just get in the van. I could just get in and go to sleep. I was so, so empty. I felt like crying; I may have even had a cry. I so nearly pulled the plug. But I didn't. I did what I needed to do – like I'd always done. I silently took off my boots, changed my socks, ate a massive bag of pretzels, drank a litre of water and a Coke, changed my top and got my head torch out. Fuck this. At this point in my running journey, I had yet to DNF. I wasn't going to do it now. The van turned up. The crew had been looking for a McDonald's. They hadn't found one.

My feet were white and wrinkled. They looked like the feet you see poking out of the end of a gurney in a crime drama. I poured rubbing alcohol on them to dry them out. I did think about drinking some, but at seventy per cent proof I'm not sure even I could manage that. I let them dry, lubed them up and hoped for the best. They were so fucking sore. I would deal with them after I had done this last section. And I *would* do this section.

I was on my own as I started running. But I was *running* now. As nice as it was to be back on roads, it wasn't so great when my head torch batteries decided to run out. My spares were in the support van. I was now running down unlit Panamanian dual carriageways, using my phone as a torch, huge lorries careering towards me blowing their horns. Autopilot. Get it done. Don't die. I was well ahead of the others. I just wanted to finish.

Turning off the dual carriageway to see the Pacific shining in the dark was amazing. It was about 9 p.m. I'd been going for almost seventeen hours, and I'd done it. I'd crossed Panama in a day. The rest of the team arrived in dribs and drabs, pale, hungry, covered in mud, blood and sweat, but overjoyed. Back at the hotel we tried to wash our kit in the showers (i.e. we trashed the hotel) and managed to get the receptionist to order us a pizza from the local takeaway. It took *ages* for the smallest pizza in the world to arrive, but with that, a hot shower and a couple of beers, all was almost forgotten. Almost.

I was caught on the high of the achievement. What we had ahead of us was going to be next-level horrendous, but I remember sitting in that hotel room with the boys feeling happy and accepted. I remember really feeling like I was in the moment, thinking, *FUCK, look at what I am capable of!* I remember that feeling so well. *They must think I am fucking great,* I thought. Did I think I was great? I sort of felt like it had happened by accident – that I'd been winging it. That I was lucky. All I cared about was what *they* thought of *me*, something I had absolutely no control over. Thinking about what other people think of you is a great way of distracting yourself from what you actually think of yourself. The irony is that, often, they are the same thing.

Early the next morning we headed to Panama City to catch a flight to the start point for the second traverse of the country. From Las Olas, the itinerary would involve two days' road running (about twenty-five to thirty miles a day), three days' self-supported hiking through primary jungle and a day's packrafting to the coast. Starting on the Pacific coast we would run about thirty miles towards Chiriqui, where we would stop for the day. On day two we'd run a further thirty miles to Totumas, which is right at the edge of the jungle. After a night in a jungle lodge, we would enter the jungle with our ridiculous backpacks and spend three days crossing it; the plan was to cover around sixteen miles a day. On day five we would emerge at the edge of the jungle, jump on packrafts and paddle towards the coast, where we would be extracted by boat and taken to Bocas del Toro, aka the Caribbean island of dreams, where we would eat, drink and be merry. The final day would be spent on the island. White beaches, food and, yes, the drinks are free. It was literally Club Tropicana.

It all looked pretty doable on paper. However, the team had been travelling, running and hiking over some pretty extreme terrain for just over two weeks with no rest days – and the first crossing had been a pretty seismic wake-up call. The jungle was slow and terrifying. Our bodies were mashed, but my brain wanted to get this done. I was 100 per cent focused on getting to that island, in it for the long haul. What followed was the most intense week of my life so far.

Having arrived at our pre-crossing hotel in the dark, the team had yet another 5 a.m. alarm call. We met on the beach as the sun was rising. I was absolutely exhausted, but semi-excited to get a bit of road running done. The sunrise was beautiful and at 7 a.m., with pelicans flying off in what appeared to be a guard of honour, we turned away from the Pacific and started the journey across Panama.

The two road days weren't that bad. I say that; sometimes I look back on stuff and say it wasn't that bad when it was frankly terrible. But on the scale of what was to come, it wasn't so bad. It was fucking hot, humid and my God it was hilly – a good 7,000–8,000 feet of vert according to my watch over the two days. We got it done. At one point, me and one of the boys decided we wanted a beer – and got one by googling pictures of beers on our phones and showing them to the guy that owned one of the many roadside shacks we ran past. I could *always* get beer. Beer is an international language.

Things had started to slide admin wise, and even by my own low standards I wasn't looking after myself very well at all. For the first two days we stayed in decent accommodation – accommodation that had proper food and a beer fridge. There were drinks to be drunk at night, so I drank them. I'd also decided that a stone I had lodged in my shoe for most of day two didn't need to be immediately removed, resulting in an almighty blister on the ball of my foot – not ideal the night before you go into a jungle. Making decisions was becoming a very difficult and slow process, especially as I was half-cut most of the time. This resulted in a couple of regrettable life choices on my part, the first being that a hydrocolloid gel blister plaster was the best course of action for that blister, and the second being the frankly haphazard packing of my sixty-five-litre jungle bag.

The blister plaster decision was just fucking stupid and led to more fluid building up pushing against the dressing. There was nothing else to do but rip it (and the top layer of skin) off my foot. I now had an open wound to take with me on my little trip. I poured iodine in it, had another sip of beer and hoped for the best.

The bag packing was a fucking joke. Everything we needed in the jungle we had to take in that bag. Everything from meals to hammocks to toilet roll. I didn't take my camp shoes, I didn't take the right food and I substituted my own gear for two cans of Red Bull for our videographer, who had no space in his bag due to camera gear. PEOPLE-PLEASING! I could go on all day about how many mistakes I made packing that bag. By the time I was done, it must have weighed thirty to thirty-five kilos. I had only ever walked from my house to the Tube with a bag that heavy – now I was crossing a country carrying it. When I put it on, I nearly fell over. Our two local guides, Moses and Elvin, laughed at me. Fair. If I hadn't been so terrified I would have laughed at me too. Why hadn't I trained to carry weight? Too late now. *It's only three days*, I told myself, uncapping yet another 'social' beer after attempting and failing to put my hammock up indoors.

Now let's be very clear about what sort of trip this was. In the jungle, there would be no support crew, no shop, no vehicle, no extra snacks, no extra water, no tent, no shower, no toilet, no phone signal, no medic, no nothing. There would be no get-outs, no going back and no trotting off on your own. We would be entirely dependent on ourselves and each other. If I wanted out, it would be via emergency helicopter, and I would need to be quite badly injured. It's a fucking serious business. I had no frame of reference for this. Even the one-day crossing had been supported. I had also not registered any of the self-talk that had been going on. I'd been dealing with it like I would back in London – by busying and drinking it away. Now there would be no busying. There would be no drinking. There would just be me, my small team and the jungle.

From the get-go, it was extremely tough going. The terrain was hard, chalky rock, mostly vertical, always wet. We all got on with it, hoofing ourselves up, trying to drink enough water and take enough salt. It was already hot, but it was manageable. I had pre-emptively taken some codeine for my foot. It didn't hurt any more, but everything else did. After a couple of hours, we got to the outskirts of the jungle. Yes, reader, that is correct, we weren't even in it yet. The first two miles had taken us twenty-eight minutes and twenty-nine minutes respectively. Those two miles were the fastest two miles we would do that day. Or all week, for that matter.

It started to get muddy. Really muddy. December is the end of rainy season in Panama, so there had been months and months of heavy rain. A year later a mudslide would occur in the very place we were standing, killing a number of locals and destroying the part of the lodge we had just left. The miles just got longer and slower. A forty-four-minute mile, a forty-nine-minute mile, a fifty-minute mile; on and on it went. Energy was sapped. We stopped for our first lunch of cold, wet, expedition meal pasta. I think that was the day we had lunch on the Continental Divide. It's pathetic that I can't remember, but I was functioning and not engaging. I had never felt so tired. Everything was heavy. The knowledge there was no bed or shelter tonight was lingering at the back of my mind. I felt like I was in some kind of fucked-up flow state.

It wasn't until nine miles in, at about 3 p.m., when we put our packs down, that I felt a true sense of how utterly depleted I was. Taking the pack off and staring at the thick jungle where we were supposed to sleep was hideous. The aim was to set up camp at 3 p.m. or 4 p.m. every day, in daylight. Today was the only day that we would actually do that. It had taken us eight hours to do nine miles. The plan was to cover almost double that after day one.

Moses and Elvin set at it, chopping down the huge vines and leaves to make space for the hammocks. I only had one successful attempt at putting my hammock up to my name – and this was in woods in Oxford on a lovely summer's day about three weeks previously. I literally couldn't remember how to do it. It took me well over an hour (and that's with help from the boys), and it looked like shit. *That'll do*, I thought, as I stared at what looked like a dog poo bag stretched between two trees.

The first time I realised that I was absolutely rancid, was as I attempted to get ready for bed. The jungle coats you in this kind of film that literally eats through your clothes and gets into your skin. Soaked from the inside, soaked from the outside. There was nowhere to sit. I couldn't take off my boots because I had nothing else to put on my feet. Swapped sandals for Red Bull, hadn't I? The jungle floor is a mixture of mud, debris, roots, spikes, killing things, and then you've got the locals: snakes, spiders and a billion ants. My feet were wet and rotting inside my boots, and now I had no way to air them.

It was extremely difficult to get changed and still keep my stuff dry. All my dry kit was in one of many dry bags – waterproof socks, some leggings to sleep in, one extra pair of pants and two tops – all to be kept dry at all times for the night so I could sleep comfortably. I desperately tried to keep this stuff off the floor and away from the already soaking tarp above my hammock. The kit I had been wearing that day – my leggings, top, socks, coat and sports bra – were soaked in sweat and river water, and my boots were wet through. And that is how they would stay. It's always wet in the jungle. These things would never dry.

My sports bra didn't come off for the entire trip. I was scared I wouldn't get it back on, so I didn't take it off. Anyone reading this who has tried to put on a sweaty sports bra after taking it off will understand my reasoning here. It would become a part of me in more ways than one.

We ate our tiny meals and at 6 p.m. it was bedtime. It's dark and noisy in the jungle. Really fucking dark, really fucking noisy and way too wet to make a fire and sing songs. We were all shattered. The noise woke me up at about 2 a.m. I was very cold. I was very scared. I didn't want to wriggle about in case my hammock fell down or something climbed in. I slept on and off until 5 a.m. And so the days went on.

I was already physically broken. Now it was a battle with my head. *I've done this before,* I thought. *I can do it again. I just need to get on with the job.* But this was different. This was very, very different. I didn't talk to anyone at all about how I was feeling. There wasn't a camp camaraderie like there had been on previous trips because we were all trying to stay alive rather than have a laugh, so there didn't seem like a right time to chat about feels. I didn't want to be a burden, and I didn't want people to know I felt broken. I thought *they* thought I was resilient and brave, and I didn't want them to think I was moaning.

Over the days that followed everything got worse. A lot worse. The terrain was indescribably difficult, like ascending a shit-covered staircase two steps at a time. The descents were worse: steep, scary and dangerous. My legs felt empty, and the weight of my pack threatened to topple me over on a minute-by-minute basis. We had no idea when the ups would stop, and sometimes they didn't for hours. Picking a line among the rocks and mud was almost impossible. The wet kit was rubbing on my skin and there were multiple rivers to get through. The cold water offered a tiny bit of respite from the searing humidity – a few seconds of freezing comfort on my hot little feet and my sore bones.

By the third day my food rations were pretty much gone, bar a bag of fruit pastilles which in my mind became more valuable than gold. Up on the ridgelines, rocks would vanish from under my feet and roll down the enormous gorges that were usually on both sides of the paths we were attempting to navigate, hidden from us by the tops of enormous trees. I had no energy, not even enough to be scared. The group got more and more quiet; the group became silent. The group spread out. All of us were doing the best we could do, but none of us were doing enough.

It was day four when I realised that we may have been in trouble. Big fucking trouble. We should have been out of the jungle by then. We were not. I had a helpful new mantra going round and round in my head: *The jungle wants to kill us.* I kept crying and I didn't know why – not massive hysterical cries, just silent sobs. I didn't stop to cry, I just let the tears roll down my face as I tried to pick the best line to get up the never-ending hills. Sometimes, because I felt like I was on my own, I just shouted, 'FUUUUUUCK', really loud, at nothing.

My legs burnt, my lungs burnt, and my brain switched from *The jungle wants to kill us* to *You could kill yourself.* It was loud and ridiculous. I thought about taking an overdose of whatever drugs I had left in order to be helicoptered out. Instead of coming and going, those thoughts stayed at the forefront of my mind, like they were totally normal. I assumed at the time they were. I looked at the rest of the team and thought they were doing OK. I was the weak one. I was holding us up. I needed them to think I was OK.

We were behind schedule in quite a formidable way. We weren't going to make it to the island. My carrot had gone. We would be in here for at least another two days, maybe three. New feelings started to happen. They were feelings of anger, disappointment, rage, fear and frustration and were directed almost entirely at myself, although I saved ten per cent of them for the trip leader and his navigation skills. I had no way of drowning these feelings or ignoring them, and I didn't want to say anything. I didn't want to make it worse for everyone else. Everyone was fucked off with it, and nobody needed to hear my bullshit as well.

You are a piece of shit, Allie. Why can you not do this? You're letting the whole team down, you useless fuck. You knew this would happen. You're the weakest one.

I tried to think of other things. Other things that would distract me and stop me from breaking. I couldn't. I didn't know how I was going to go on. We spent a night on the porch of a tiny shack that appeared like a mirage from nowhere. We bargained with the Panamanian family that called it home, and they allowed us to sleep on the raised veranda. There were huge spiders everywhere, and no space to hang a hammock. We slept rolled in the hammocks on the floor. This tiny family, who had nothing, let us use all they had. Their children had never seen a car or a television. They didn't know what the internet was. They looked at us like we were comedy aliens. They appeared cheerful – content with what they had. They were truly living in the moment. They didn't care about the shit that I thought was important. They didn't even know about the existence of half of it. In a way I was jealous of them. I wondered if they ever felt mental pain like I did. I wondered if I had brought it all on myself.

I felt ashamed of the comforts I was missing. I felt embarrassed that even though I was privileged enough to be here on this trip I could ruin it for myself by feeling so shit. I felt angry at myself. I wanted to pull my own hair out and scratch at my skin until it bled. I now know that the only way that I could have calmed these feelings would have been to have talked to someone about them, but I didn't. Everyone else was busy looking at maps or eating dinner or trying to make their bed. There was an uneasy atmosphere I didn't want to stir up.

At the time I thought they were all super strong, dealing with it in a really admirable way, and I wanted to be like them. I now wonder what would have happened if we had all had a full and frank discussion about how we were really feeling rather than just muttering to each other that it was really hard and we were tired and we should go this way or that way. There was no room for honest, outright vulnerability on that trip. There should always be room for that.

My anxiety and fear gave way to a wave of Fucking Depression™. Fucking Depression™ didn't even knock on the door, he just kicked it in and sat on my chest. The illness started talking. I felt terrified. Suddenly the jungle wasn't the problem any more. I was.

The trip that I'd had in my head for the last four months had changed beyond recognition. That was a huge trigger for me. The thing I had been promised (my day on the beach), had been taken away. In my mind it had been taken away because I wasn't good enough. I wasn't fast enough or fit enough. It was my fault. I wanted to stop, for it to be over, but my hand was being forced. There was no way out but forwards. There was nothing I could do to medicate the noise and no end in sight. It was time for me to lean in to those thoughts, but I didn't know how. I had to accept what was actually going on. No more, 'I just want to feel better.' Now it was time to say, 'This is what is happening and I accept that.' But I didn't know how. These were excruciating, painful and incredibly difficult days.

My frame of reference had narrowed so much. My reality was different. My world was in this jungle, in the here and now. My phone, my lifeline to distraction and outside, was now just a wet camera. Alcohol was gone. My crutch. My friend. My comforter. There was nothing to distract me from me, but this time I didn't know when it was going to end. That feeling was both terrifying and in hindsight exhilarating. There was no escape from the horror of the jungle or the horror of my own thoughts. I had to face my brain and sit or walk or sleep with it.

It made me see the contradictory nature of my illness for what it was. I could tell myself I wasn't enough until I was blue in the face, but I was getting this done, no matter how slowly, and I was kind of semi-aware of that. The terrible things that my brain said about me were not happening. I was getting it done, even though I was telling myself I would never do it. This was not easy, but it was the only choice I had.

So much happened on this trip that I just can't go into here because, well, word count. But we did get out of that jungle. We didn't complete the trip as we'd planned, but we got out.

I got through those days, where my brain was more of a threat to me than the environment, intact. I don't know what the alternative would have been, but I do know that I thought about severely injuring myself in order to be medivacked out more than once. When I had those thoughts in the real world, I self-medicated them until they went away. But in Panama I couldn't. I was forced to live with them for days and days. While Panama was undoubtedly the hardest thing I have ever done, it was also one of the most important. That trip was proof that my thoughts alone could not kill me, it was only my actions that could do that *if* I allowed them to. And I hadn't. The experience had shown me that I didn't have to believe everything that I thought. I could move through those thoughts, however painful, and come out the other side. As important as these learnings were, they were forgotten the minute that first beer was opened. And that first beer was opened the second we got to a shop that sold it. *Thank fuck that's over*, I thought.

When I got home, my lovely new boyfriend came to meet me at the airport. I'd thought that I would walk through arrivals looking like some sort of bronzed GI Jane-type action woman. As it was, I had lost a stone and was pale, spotty and completely exhausted, like a sweaty little jungle ghost. He took me back to his house in Somerset – back to my home comforts and my wine. I spent a few days in shock, I think, that I had managed to get through that. I felt like I couldn't talk to him about it because he wouldn't understand. Nobody would understand unless they'd been there; I mean, I didn't understand what to take from it. Something had happened in there and I wasn't sure what. It hurt my brain to try to work it out. So I tried to carry on as usual.

Was I more grateful for what I had? Hell, fucking yes. Was I a changed person? No – but something had changed. I felt like I needed more of whatever it was that had happened in that jungle.

CHAPTER 5
LOVE IS A FOUR-LETTER WORD

Listen to: 'Song for Zula' – Phosphorescent

I always thought that love was transactional. You give someone something and you get something back. And because I didn't think I was enough, because I thought I was a broken mess, for a really long time I felt like I had nothing worth giving. I was a drain. Love was dependent on me being enough, and I'd proved in previous relationships that wasn't the case. I had no idea that love could be unconditional. I didn't even think familial love came without its conditions.

I met Julius in April 2018. We got together when I was absolutely hammered at a race in Dorset. The event was lapped, which meant I could 'socially' drink beer every lap until I could forget about the fact I hated myself and wanted to die, and also forget I was supposed to be running a marathon. My mum turned up to see me that day. I know she was intensely upset about the state I was in. I told her I was fine. I told her I was having fun. I was not fine. I was not having fun. I was shitfaced. Sorry, Mum.

Julius was lovely, and he had dogs. On this occasion, he was running with the dogs and offered me one – George – to run with. I was thrilled. I didn't particularly fancy Julius, but he seemed to be interested in what I had to slur at him, and he let me run with his dog, so we hit it off.

After that race, Julius asked me out. I was very hungover, so I said yes. I didn't want to upset him, and he was very handsome. I'm really sorry this isn't the love story that you want, dear reader, but that's how it happened. Julius is one of the kindest and most wonderful humans in my life. I now know that and treasure it. At the time I just thought, *This will do*.

Julius lived in Somerset in a little cottage with his dogs and his son. BINGO. That was my out. I would spend weekends away from London in his little house, and he would come up to London and see me when he could. We both liked running, we both liked dogs and we both *loved* a drink. He thought I was social and fun. I thought he was an idiot for coming anywhere near me. I was very, very clear with Julius about the way I felt. I remember telling him on a trip to Devon shortly after we got together that even though we were a couple and I liked him very much, I was in love with someone else (because I was), and if that person ever decided he wanted to run away with me, I would. In the same conversation, I told Julius that, regardless, I would probably end up breaking his heart and that he was definitely Mr Right Now as opposed to Mr Right. He literally took this unblinking, on the chin. I don't know if he thought he could change my mind, but he agreed to carry on as before. I'd literally just briefed him that I was a cunt, yet there he was, same as before.

Julius is completely different to any man I have ever had a relationship with – before or since. He was raised by women, and I used to joke he was more of a girl than me. He is kind, caring, thoughtful and he loves unconditionally. When I met him, I was a state; it was obvious. I had dealt with the breakdowns of 2017 by signing them off, brushing them under the carpet and thinking, *Well, that's happened now, it won't happen again*, without asking why or how it had happened. The running was ever increasing. Between the Autumn 100 in October 2017 and the Bad Cow Marathon where I met Julius in April 2018, I had run another twenty-six marathons and ultras. I was using it as a plaster to cover the cracks. The more cracks there were, the more plasters I needed. Because I felt good when I was doing it, I began to attach my entire self-worth to it. I was mistaking being someone that runs with being a runner. It had started to become my entire personality – another kind of cover story to hide behind.

When I wasn't running, I felt like shit. The blogs on my website detailing those races make me cringe. They're basically, 'LOOK AT ME, I AM THE WORLD'S GREATEST ULTRARUNNER and I am doing JUST FINE!' but are peppered with pictures of me drinking and comments about how much I could drink. Boast posts. I had to drink to get through what little life I was living outside of running, and addiction doesn't just stop for a fifty-mile ultra.

Meeting Julius was a bit of a shocker. I couldn't believe someone could be so kind to someone that was so obviously fucked up. He supported me at every event I did. One of our first dates saw him pacing me on a seventy-five-mile ultramarathon. About twenty minutes after he'd started running with me, I decided I needed a poo and ended up shouting at him to 'bring me Vaseline' from a bush, with my shorts around my ankles. He did it. He didn't bat an eyelid. He would drive for hours to crew me or pick me up. He told me he thought I was wonderful. He encouraged me, laughed at my shit jokes and took me out for drinks and dinners. He showed me what it was to be loved for being me, no matter how much of a lunatic I thought I was. He never had a go at me or told me how to behave or what to change. He accepted me as I was, and he absolutely loved me regardless. I think he could see through it all. I think he thought he could change it. I need to ask him about that.

I would spend hours on the phone to him when we were apart – mainly drunk crying, talking about how awful I felt and letting him kindly talk me off the ledge. When we went out together, it was super fun. Sometimes I'd forget how much of a twat I was and how much I hated myself. We ran loads of events together, him slowing down so I could keep up with him and me telling him off for talking too much. We were together whenever we could be; he was a very welcome distraction, but something wasn't right. My thoughts ping-ponged between *I don't deserve this* and *I am going to fuck this up*.

Before moving in with Julius I was living alone in a tiny studio flat in Muswell Hill. I'd had to move out of the flat I'd shared with Cat because she was about to start trying for babies and it was just time to go. I was pretty distraught, but found myself a tiny, overpriced hellhole where I could drink whenever I wanted and crack on with pretending to piece my life together. I was desperately trying to get my business to go in a different direction. I loved running, and I wanted to do less music industry stuff, so I'd taken on a couple of wellness clients and was doing some marketing for them. I was also doing some freelance stuff for the events company I had been to Mongolia with, and the Namibia and Panama plans were afoot. I felt some kind of hope, but in drowning the bad thoughts I also poisoned the good ones. I was anxious and scared most of the time.

I longed to leave London, and meeting Julius had only made me want to leave more. But London had become my whole identity. It had seeped into my skin like an abusive partner, telling me that it loved me one minute then fucking me over the next. Everything in me wanted to leave, but I had no idea how to do it. I was terrified to let go, terrified to make a change like that, terrified it would look like failing. It was all about what other people thought. I didn't spare a thought for myself. And then someone else came into my life. Someone that changed everything. Ladies and Gentlemen, please be upstanding for the light of my life, the love of my life and the motherfucking greatest, Ms Pickle Pie.

In February 2018, news reached me that one of my friends had had a brain aneurysm in a yoga class. I know. What the actual fuck? I *knew* yoga was bad for you. I had known KP for years through music; she was pretty high-flying, very well respected but also super nice and we would hang out in the same bars, pubs and at gigs. She was one of my many shoulders to cry on at work and just an excellent person to have in my life. She has seen me in some shit-awful states and got me out of trouble more than once, and for that I am truly grateful – cheers, Kapers. To this day she is one of my greatest friends, and I don't have loads of those.

The aneurysm was pretty serious, and, as KP also worked for herself, had a huge impact on both her ability to work and her social life. It took her months and months to recover from an operation that has a pretty low survival rate, but recover she did. As she slowly started to rehabilitate, we spent more and more time together. She was frustrated about the fact she couldn't remember things, that she had no sense of taste or smell and that she was really struggling to get back into work.

A few years earlier during a 'Fuck my life, what am I doing?' moment, I'd volunteered on a shark research vessel in South Africa. I'd spent four weeks out there, working with a research team observing great white sharks in their natural habitat, cage diving and explaining to the general public that if we did kill every shark in the ocean, we would also die pretty quickly. At the time, that trip helped reset me (yet another plaster stuck on what was a pretty seriously broken bone), and I suggested that maybe KP think about doing something similar. I wanted her to go and live life and do the simple things for a bit. I thought it would help. Long story short, she saw a Facebook post featuring a puppy called Lucy and ended up shipping out to Bulgaria for three weeks to work in a stray dog sanctuary.

KP didn't like dogs. She was scared of dogs. But she had forgotten this because of the aneurysm. The fact she couldn't smell or taste anything also meant she was good for all the shit jobs – literally. I was super chuffed she was doing something away from the stress of normal life and really hoped that it would help her. I had no idea how much it would help me.

KP had been at the sanctuary for about a week when a message popped up on my phone. It was a photo of a puppy. A scraggy, fluffy puppy with massive feet, huge eyes and scabs all over its head. It was the same puppy as the one in the video that had convinced KP to go. The puppy called Lucy. My heart stopped. My first thought was, *That's my dog.*

Looking at that picture sent a lightning bolt through me. I can't explain the feeling. It was like I knew this dog. It was like I had seen her before. That was *my* dog. I was not in the market for a dog, I was not looking for a dog, I was not in the right situation in my life to have a dog, but here was *my* dog, staring back at me from my phone. My message back was literally, 'CAN I HAVE HER?'

I spoke to Julius. I couldn't do this on my own. We hatched a plan. She would live part-time with me in London and part-time with him in Somerset. I had no garden. I had no money. My flat was one room. I was a functioning alcoholic depressive with debts coming out of my ears and a penchant for running away at any given opportunity. This was an incredibly stupid decision on all fronts. But I couldn't stop thinking about her. *My* dog.

Lucy had been found at the side of the road. The sanctuary thought she was dead so had approached her with a body bag, but when they picked her up her little heart was still beating, so they took her in. They removed the thousands of ticks from her and began to rehabilitate her. The theory is she was thrown from a passing lorry or refuse truck. She still hates refuse trucks now. I didn't want her to have a human name, so I called her Pickle. Her colouring was the same as a jar of Branston Pickle. I don't know where the Pie bit came from, but that was her name. Pickle Pie. Julius and I picked her up from South Mimms services on 16 August 2018 – the day before my birthday.

In Allie's Great Fun Dream World™, I would get to the pick-up point and she would bound out of the van towards me, jump into my arms licking my face, and immediately my life would be a million times better. The reality was very, very different. She was terrified. She had spent three days travelling across the EU in a van. When they opened the crate, she refused to get out. When they managed to get her out, she hid under the van. She was tiny, thin, stinky and extremely scared. I started to cry. Julius wrapped her up in a towel we had brought with us, and we put her in the car. I got in the boot with her. I cried and cried. She looked at me. She was so broken. *I* was so broken. What had I done? She could hardly stand up and was shaking. I held her. I looked at her. I felt this surge of ridiculous love. I promised her that I would look after her and love her for the rest of her life. I held her all the way back to my flat and cried.

The following weeks were awful. Pickle was so incredibly fragile that I couldn't really take her anywhere. She was terrified of London. All she had known was the sanctuary. She had never been anywhere like London. She was terrified of the noise, buses, people, other dogs. We had straight away introduced her to Julius's dogs – Toby and George – both of whom immediately took a liking to her and welcomed her into the pack. They looked after her and looked out for her for the first few days, but once Julius had gone back to Somerset, I was left with this wreck of a puppy with no idea how to look after her. I couldn't leave her alone, so I would try to take her to the pub with me. She hated it and cowered, shaking under the chairs. I tried to take her to work with me; she hated the Tube, she hated the bus, she wouldn't walk down the street – I had to carry her.

The only time she was happy was when she was running around Highgate Woods with me. I took her running about two weeks after I got her – absolutely the wrong thing to do to a four-to-five-month-old puppy, I know this now. I would slowly run five kilometres with her on the lead round the park, and in that time she would come to life. She *loved* running, and I loved her for loving it. When she was running, all the fear vanished. She would bop along next to me, she would look at me, we would have the best thirty minutes of the day together. But the minute the running stopped she shrank back into herself, and I would have to carry her home. Being with that dog was like being with my own brain in hairy four-legged form.

It didn't get any better. I was at my wits' end. I felt so guilty for bringing Pickle into my life on what appeared to be a whim. I hated London for making her feel like this. I hated London for making *me* feel like this. I hired a dog psychologist who came round to the flat and told me that she didn't think I had time for this dog and should consider giving her back. I paid her £80 to tell me that, and nearly punched her in the face. I think that was the day the decision was made. I had to take Pie out of London. This was no longer about me, it was about *us*. We both needed to move out of London. So we made a plan. As soon as I got back from Namibia and Panama we were going.

It was so much easier to make that decision when I had a reason staring me in the face. *I'm doing it for Pickle. I'm doing it for Pie.* She was so much happier in Somerset. Whenever we went to see Julius, she came out of her shell. She *loved* Julius. She still does. Pickle doesn't really get on with men as a general rule, and I questioned this with KP, who told me that Pickle had only known kindness from women because only women worked at the sanctuary at the time.

The first man to show her kindness was Julius, and she loved him for it. *Touchée*, Pie. *Touchée*.

In January 2019, a month after I returned from Panama, Julius drove a van to my flat. I filled it up with all my stuff and we drove out of London for the last time. I cried and cried. I was relieved. I was grateful. I was saved. I was running away from that old life, those thoughts, feelings, memories, the depression, the anxiety, the mistakes, the 'old me'. I was leaving it all there. This was the change that needed to happen. This was the one the doctors and my mum had told me to make. This was what would make me happy forever. I really hoped I wouldn't mess it up.

I had a bit of downtime when I first got to Somerset. I had a tiny bit of money in the bank and so took a month to get used to my new surroundings. I remember thinking, *This is an amazing opportunity, don't fuck this up*, about ten times a day. I now had a partner, three dogs, a part-time actual human child and a home in the countryside. I bought a car (my first car, Cecil the money-pit Mini, at the age of thirty-eight …). I'd done it. I'd got the dream. Don't fuck it up.

I went to the pub and got shitfaced to celebrate.

2019 was the year when I thought that I'd done it, I had managed to change all the things that had 'made' me sad. I had worked through the depression in the jungle and literally come out the other side. I had dealt with it and wouldn't need to do that again. It was all over. I still got depressed, but I could distract myself from it with a few drinks and my lovely boyfriend and dogs and my simple life in the countryside. More adventures were being planned. I was working closely with the events company I had been on previous trips with, and we were planning more and more trips for the coming years. I was able to make half a living doing this, and half a living with a part-time job in Bristol. The events company sent Julius and me to Malta to test an event running across all three islands that make up that incredible country. They sent me to Scotland to traverse the width of the country on foot and by kayak, and they sent me to the Outer Hebrides to run the Hebridean Way – 156 miles from the southernmost tip of Vatersay to the Butt of Lewis in the very north – another world first. No other group had run this route in the way that we planned to do it, and for that trip I chose an all-female team. I had become really aware of the low numbers of women taking part in ultra-distance races and I wanted to make a point; I wanted to show that women could do this stuff, that they were brave, fierce and more than capable. To this day that's one of the trips I am most proud of being part of.

I had adventures in the UK with Julius and Pickle too, running multiple marathons and ultras including the 112-mile Devon Coast to Coast, the Ultra Tour of Arran and Centurion Running's legendary Piece of String race. The latter has no route, no distance and no plan. You turn up and do what you're told. Absolute head-fuck of an event. I became only the second woman to have ever finished it. I was instrumental in organising a team of forty people to break a Guinness World Record running the York Marathon in a Viking boat costume, and I returned to Namibia to help crew the first public outing of Race to the Wreck – the event that I had tested the year before. Watching that event come together was incredible; it filled me with pride and joy that I had been part of the first team to go out and check the route and that now I was bringing that experience to other people. I saw that event change people's lives. I am still mates with a lot of the clients that went on that trip. We still talk about the power of it now.

Pickle would come and run marathons and ultras with me when the event allowed it, and when it didn't Julius would look after her. She once ran the entire circumference of the Isle of Wight in two days for fun. She loved running as much as I did. She loved me. She loved me because I was her mum, regardless of anything I had done, the messes I'd made or the thoughts that I had. She loved me. And my God did I love her.

The time I spent living outside of London with Julius and Pickle and the other dogs was making me better. Julius and Pickle's love for me appeared to be completely unconditional. No matter how low I was, no matter how sad I got, both of them picked me up and comforted me. Both of them cared for and loved me for who I really was and allowed me the space that I needed to do what I wanted to do. Julius encouraged me to pursue the work with the events company and supported me when I went on mega-long trips away. Julius and Pickle saw the best of me and the worst of me, yet they were always there. Julius is still one of the only people in the world (apart from a few members of my family) who actually knows me to the very bones of me. He's a truly incredible person.

This part of my life was almost a rebuild phase. I had catastrophised leaving London for so long, but nothing bad had happened when I did; in fact only good things had happened. My drinking, although still every day, was different; now I was doing it for pleasure rather than to numb pain – or so I told myself. Things were going well. I had a routine dictated by Pickle and work. I could talk to Pickle about anything, and regardless of what I said, she loved me. I loved watching her develop into this confident, happy, fit dog. *I've done that*, I thought. *I am giving her the life she deserves*. Pickle has always had underlying behavioural issues – she still has some – but I just celebrated the good things that were happening (a lot like I did with myself) and ignored the problems.

I had all the things I'd wanted, but as positively as life was moving forward and as much as I tried to ignore it, there was something I was not addressing. I absolutely loved Julius, but I was not *in love* with him. And that made me incredibly uneasy.

Instead of talking to him about it, instead of dealing with it as I should have done, I distracted myself from it and hoped it would get better – in the same way I had distracted myself from other things and hoped they would get better. I drank. We drank. We went out a lot to the pub, we drank at home. It's way easier to pretend you are in love with someone when you're drunk. We weren't out-of-control-drinking-in-the-morning drinkers – we had jobs and responsibilities and we both worked hard – but every night we would open a bottle of wine 'to unwind' in front of the TV. Then maybe open another one. At one point we *both* gave up drinking for six months. I can't remember why, but when we started again it was explosive.

During those six sober months it became obvious something was missing. We were both pretending that we hadn't noticed it. The night we *did* start drinking again we had an incredibly vicious fight about why we hadn't really been having sex for the last few months.

The fight lasted seventy-two hours. He never did get an answer to that question. Not until it was too late.

There were a couple of things going on here. It infuriated me that he was so docile with me. I was almost annoyed that he didn't pick holes in me like my previous partners had. It infuriated me that he could love me so much despite all my flaws. I had never, ever experienced that from a partner before, and it felt weird. I could literally do no wrong. Is this what love is? I still don't know. I couldn't accept it. I didn't believe him when he told me how brilliant he thought I was. I thought he was saying it out of desperation to keep me with him. Fucking harsh. But that's what I thought.

I was not in love with Julius, and I wasn't honest about that. I loved him from the bottom of my heart – still do. But I was not *in love* with him, despite what I might have told him at the time. I thought if I said it, it would make it happen. It doesn't work like that, and I hated myself for it. I loved being around him, living with him and thought he was extremely handsome and kind. I acted like I *was* in love with him because that's what I thought he wanted me to do. That's what I thought I had to give back in exchange for his love for me. I kept telling myself that this was what I'd always wanted, and I didn't want to fuck it up, but I just couldn't see forever with him. Even my mum told me not to fuck it up. She loved Julius; she still does. I remember her saying to me, 'Don't you break that man's heart', and being very serious about it. I knew I would meet someone else. I knew I would break his heart. And then I did.

I first met That Person in October 2019. I can't remember exactly when it was that That Person told me they were married, but it was fairly early on, and before anything had happened between us. I was disappointed, I'll be honest, but it is what it is, right? We could just be mates. I had a boyfriend at home anyway.

The more I got to know That Person, the more we talked about stuff, the more I liked them. They told me they weren't happy at home. They told me their marriage was all but over. We were mates. We confided in each other about life and hopes and dreams. We rolled our eyes at the same things. We laughed at the same stuff. We liked the same bands. We both liked a drink.

We both said, 'I don't usually do this sort of thing.' But we did it. I felt awful about it. But I was completely intoxicated. In more ways than one. I felt like I was head over heels in love.

I went home and told Julius I had met someone else. I didn't say who it was, but I told him I had met someone, and I had feelings for them. I didn't tell him what had happened, and I didn't break up with him. In fact, I told him nothing had happened. That was a lie. He was heartbroken. I fell into a well of self-pity, guilt and anger at myself tinged with the fact I thought I was in love with someone who was married. In love. What even is that? I'd only met them a few times. I got very, very depressed, very quickly. I started to drink very heavily – it was Christmas after all. I became more and more distant with Julius. I arranged to meet That Person in London just before Christmas to 'go over what had happened'. We got drunk. It happened again. This time it was worse for many, many reasons.

Things progressed rapidly over the following months. We started making plans to be together as a proper couple. Hundreds of messages exchanged. Hundreds of promises and excited plans for the future. That Person would tell me I was the love of their life on an almost daily basis, and I would tell them the same. I'd never felt like this about anyone. I felt like this was the final piece of the puzzle sliding right into place.

It was like being in a bubble. I tried not to ask when they would tell their partner because it would ruin the mood. It was getting sorted, they would say. Now wasn't the right time, they would say. For many, many months I believed we were doing things the right way. We weren't. We fucking weren't.

I cannot begin to tell you the shame I feel writing this now, or how much I wish it didn't happen, but it did. I can make excuses – I have a whole list of them – but I don't want to excuse myself, that's not respectful to the people I hurt. This shit happens all the time, everywhere. I just didn't think I would ever be involved in it; nobody ever does, I don't think.

I felt like an incredibly bad person for a really, really long time. I was stupid, naive, inconsiderate, selfish; I'm sure you can think of a whole range of adjectives to insert here – and feel free to do that. I used to do that all the time, judge other people's behaviour – until it happened to me. Judging people is very easy, but before you *do* judge my behaviour, make sure yours is perfect first. I now live by that rule.

I remembered my dad lying, and I didn't want to lie to people I loved. I knew I needed to tell Julius. So I did. And it was terrible. But I did what I needed to do. I made myself a free agent, just as I believed That Person would.

Julius was incredible. He told me he knew, that he had guessed, that he was grateful for my honesty. I was still living in Somerset with him and knew I would have to move out. But something else was going on. COVID was here.

A few of my work trips with the events company had been postponed or changed. There was some kind of virus flying about and certain countries had shut borders or were refusing UK travellers. Everything was a bit weird. And it was about to get a whole lot weirder.

After I'd told Julius about That Person, I decided to give him some space. I booked myself into a little cottage in the Lake District and took Pickle with me. I was there, on 23 March 2020, when the national lockdown was announced.

Like everyone else on earth, I was terrified. I couldn't be forced to stay at home, I was a runner. How would I get to see That Person? What would happen to us? What would happen with my work? I was doing more and more for the events company, and I could almost see a future doing just that. 'This time next year we'll be living together,' That Person texted, the week before lockdown was announced. At the time even I thought that was a bit soon …

In the meantime, Julius and I would need to be able to live together for a while longer. I went back to Somerset and moved into the spare room. Julius and I agreed to make the best of things – and he was brilliant. At the end of the day, we were *great* friends. The fact I had come clean meant we could now start to rebuild some trust and work on our friendship. If he hated me, he was doing a very good job of hiding it. We shared the home schooling and got heavily involved with *PE with Joe*. My running actually accelerated, and I got super fit. Living in the middle of nowhere meant that my one bit of exercise a day became a four-hour-long run. That first lockdown was made good by having the man who would become my best friend living with me, the love of my life making plans for the future over text and me doing *a lot* of running.

As COVID ebbed and flowed I saw That Person as much as I could without making it obvious. The excuses came thick and fast from their end. They couldn't tell their partner about their future plans because that would make living arrangements difficult. I agreed. I believed they had a plan. Every time there was a lull in lockdowns we would go somewhere. Every time we did that, more and more plans were made. I kept everything secret. *I was* a secret. Every time we spoke, they told me they were a bit closer to telling their partner. When we couldn't see each other, we'd have date nights on Zoom. It was absolutely going to happen. I just had to be patient. So I was.

Apart from this pandemic malarky, the future was looking pretty bright. I was hoping I could maintain this incredible friendship I had with Julius and hoping to get more work with the events company; the work I was doing with them was going well. Although we couldn't go anywhere now, we were making big plans for future events – and booking people on to them. Because of the issues with leaving the UK, we decided to think about what we could do inside the UK. We came up with an idea that I thought was incredible: an event that allowed people to run from Land's End to John o'Groats (LEJOG) on trails and road. We started planning a 1,000-mile, five-week epic covering the entire country on some of the best trails and public rights of way in the UK. It sounded insane. It was insane. I planned accommodation for every night and got a team of fifteen people to agree to come with me and do it in September 2020; we thought the lockdowns would be done by then. They weren't. It was postponed.

While it wasn't ideal, I was busy planning ahead, I was making the best of a very shit situation and I told myself I was happy, I was moving forward. I wasn't even drinking as much those days. Too much to do. Too many plans to make. That Person still hadn't told their partner about me. This caused some pretty huge arguments between us, but I reasoned that they knew what they were doing, and I was just putting too much pressure on them. Because that's what they told me. What's that I can see flapping about on the horizon? Oh, it looks like a massive red flag. That's annoying, it's blocking the view of my perfect life. I'll ignore it.

In September 2020, I was offered a full-time job with the events company. I was over the moon. They would create a role for me that meant that I would be going out and testing these incredible routes full-time. I would be working with the events team all the time and being paid for it. This was literally a dream come true. I would have to move north, to where the company was based. It also happened to be near where That Person was based. They were so, so happy for me. They were so, so proud of me. This was it. I honestly can't remember being happier than I was at that point. I really do believe that the few days after I got that job were the happiest of my life. Everything was coming together. Everything was making sense. I felt like I was standing on the edge of the world, waiting to jump off.

And I was.

CHAPTER 6
THERE IS A ROCK BOTTOM

Listen to: 'Exile' – Taylor Swift feat. Bon Iver

The move was a really big deal. My family and my small circle of running mates all lived down south. That was where my support network was. I would be almost five hours away from all of them once in Yorkshire. A move up north would mean that not only would I be living alone again, but I would be without Pickle. The nature of the work that the events company wanted me to do meant that I would be away a lot. It was a compromise I was willing to make – a huge compromise that I was dreading. With Julius living in Somerset and nobody that I knew in the north to help, it just wasn't feasible to take her, but it was temporary. When things settled down, she would come up and live with me; it would only be for a few months, maximum. My heart ached. But I needed to move out. I needed to give Julius his space. I needed to start my new life.

That Person was incredibly helpful. They told me that once I was up north, they would introduce me to their friends, some of whom had dogs too, and eventually, when we moved in together, it wouldn't be a problem having someone to look after her. They told me where to look for a flat. They told me on a weekly basis how we would soon be 'a proper couple' and build a house made of old shipping containers.

For now, I was looking for a flat on my own; I didn't want to move in with anyone. I needed my own space. All this stuff with That Person was pretty stressful. I felt super sorry for them. They still hadn't said anything about me to their partner, despite their partner guessing that something was going on between us multiple times. When they said they didn't want to break their partner's trust, I pointed out that they *were* breaking their trust and needed to tell them the truth. We would have full-on arguments about it, where we wouldn't speak for days. A few months previously, when I was still living in Somerset, they had called me, saying that they were newly single. It was an odd call, but they told me that the deed was done, and the relationship was over. They told me that when asked, they had explicitly said there was nobody else involved. Again. I didn't like this at all but accepted it. Motivated bias: I wanted things to be the way I wanted them so I accepted the unacceptable. I did this the whole way through the 'relationship'.

They ended the call by asking me out on our first real date, and I said yes – totally thrilled. I didn't know when that date would be, but regardless they had asked me on it. Things were moving forward. We were going to be a real couple. Them not being honest with their now ex-partner was the only thing we really argued about. I told them that if their ex-partner ever asked me direct, I would tell them the truth. And I meant it.

I told That Person everything about myself: I told them all my triggers, about my mental health, about my fear of being abandoned, about my relationship history. They listened to me, took it all in and expressed acute anger that I could feel so shit about myself. They told me I was wonderful. That made me calm. It made me trust them. They sent me gifts in the post. They told me they had never met anyone like me, that I was incredible, amazing, brilliant. I believed them. I absolutely believed them – why would I not? Life was just starting for me. The time I spent with That Person was so magical and so intoxicating that I often forgot about the immense secret they were hiding. I think they did too.

Finding somewhere to live was hard work; I just couldn't find anywhere I could afford or liked. I was really scared of living alone again, despite the fact that That Person constantly reassured me they would be there, their friends would be there, and we would be this 'proper couple'. I had my reasons for being scared. When I was up north working or flat hunting, their behaviour was shady as fuck. They were paranoid they would get 'found out'. If we met up, it was for minutes. The first date did not materialise. Something wasn't right. But I wanted to believe it would be OK. I was told it would be OK. So I cracked on. I just had to be patient. I just had to be brave. The more this went on, the more anxious I got. But I knew how to deal with this. Wine. My old friend wine.

I had sort of stopped eating and replaced food with wine. Because wine blocked out all the noise. *Just get through these tough bits and it will be OK*, I thought. *Have a drink*. So I did have a drink. Lots of drinks. I didn't totally acknowledge what I was doing. It was just a stressful time. That Person continually told me not to put pressure on them. When I voiced my concerns, I was told more than once that I was being dramatic. My dad used to say the same. Dramatic wasn't a good thing in my book. I felt like I was being told off, that it was all my fault.

I eventually found a flat that looked OK. There was a very strict 'no dogs allowed' rule and it didn't have any outdoor space. But it was all I could find and all I could afford. It was weird pandemic times, and I didn't even view it before I moved in. I just found it and took it. It was a shop conversion which had been done quite badly. It had one window at the front that looked out on to the street. It was very small, but it would do; I wouldn't even be there much anyway, I'd be away working most of the time. Living my fucking great life.

At the end of October 2020, Julius once again packed the van and drove me to my new home. He did so with that unconditional love and immense fear for my well-being. He thought I was making a mistake and he had been quite vocal about it. He thought that, but he supported me anyway. When I got there, That Person came round for five minutes about an hour after we arrived. They didn't want anyone to see they were there. I spent my first night in that flat alone. Which was good practice for how I would spend every other night in it. Alone.

Despite it looking earlier in the month like the lockdowns were coming to an end, they did not. As soon as I moved in, the rule of six was cancelled, the curfews came back in, pubs and cafes shut, and a new national lockdown was announced. I was effectively imprisoned. I had no internet in my house and no phone signal. Because my flat was a conversion, various issues had meant they couldn't get a phone line in. I would have to wait, and it could take weeks. There was no radio signal either. I had no way of watching television, talking to anyone or distracting myself from being alone. *It will be OK,* I told myself, *I'll have internet soon.* I spent the evenings drinking wine and texting That Person from the smallest corner of the living room where I occasionally got signal. The texts back were getting less frequent. When they did come back, they were shorter. It wasn't the same.

I could still go to work because I couldn't work from home with no Wi-Fi. Work was a thirty-five-minute drive away. I would stop off for a ready meal and a bottle of wine on the way home every single night. Most nights the ready meal would go in the bin. I wasn't hungry. It would be OK. That Person still hadn't told their partner. The reasons came thick and fast. I believed them because I trusted them. I had to wait. I felt sick. I drank more wine. I kept the curtains on the one window I had permanently closed.

I was going to work, but work was scary too. We were an events company. There were no events. I was tired, hungry and hungover most of the time. I was under pressure sales wise, and I didn't like being in the office because I felt like everyone knew what a mess I was. I was starting to get paranoid. I tried to perform. I tried to keep the two things separate, but it was impossible. The only 'friends' I had up north were my work colleagues. I did confide in some of them, but it was weird and not appropriate. I felt so fucking lonely. It was all so horrendously entangled. It was all so horrendously shit.

The various lockdowns meant that most of the time I couldn't travel back to Somerset to see Pickle legally. I felt trapped. After five weeks I still didn't have any internet or phone signal. It was taking ages. I only saw That Person outside of my house and outside of my village briefly. There had been no date. It was because of lockdown, they said. The future, the future, the future. When we are a real couple. I waited. I was incredibly anxious. I needed my friends. I needed my family. *No, be brave, this is the future that you've always wanted. You'll be back to travelling soon.* I drank at least a bottle and a half of wine every single night to numb the feelings that something terrible was going to happen – that something terrible *was* happening. I always kept half a bottle in the fridge to prove that I could take it or leave it. *Be brave, go to sleep, Allie.* I missed my dog so much that it is impossible to put it into words. I started taking the sleeping pills I'd been given by the crisis workers the first time around. I'd started getting my mum to get them from the pharmacy and post them to me in bulk because they wouldn't give them to me in Sainsbury's. I cried a lot. I felt so ill, mentally, physically, just so ill. I felt embarrassed. I couldn't get ill again; it was shameful. The mask went on every morning, but by lunchtime it was slipping.

Months started to pass. Things got worse. That Person would say they were going to come round and then either not come at all or turn up for five minutes and leave because they said they felt guilty. Sometimes I would beg them to stay. I would literally get on my knees, in tears, and beg them to stay. Sexy. They never stayed. In the nine months I lived in that flat they stayed over once and left at 4 a.m. so nobody would see them. I would get extremely drunk and send them relationship-ending texts from the only spot in the living room that got reception. I would beg them to tell their partner. They would tell me they could do without the drama in their life. In some part of my brain, it was dawning on me I was going backwards. I'd felt like this before. I was back to exactly where I had been fifteen years ago in London. Lonely, drunk and being controlled. What the fuck had happened? I needed to get a grip. They were right. I was dramatic. I was a pathetic, demanding cunt. That's the only word I can use to describe how I felt. I felt like a cunt.

I would still go running. It was automatic. I ran a lot. I felt nothing when I ran. I started to get scared about the routes I chose in case I bumped into someone I shouldn't. I did some pretty big races during this time as well – the ones that I could do between lockdowns. Fifty-milers, 100-milers. I actually found them easier than I do now. Because I felt nothing on them. No pain, no nothing. It was just running by numbers. I was on absolute autopilot. Running was doing nothing for me at all at this point. Nothing was.

I would sometimes speak to Julius about the situation. I would sometimes speak to my friend Lorna about it. I knew what they thought; they thought it was a waste of time. They were gravely concerned about my well-being, but I wanted to believe it would be OK. They listened to me and supported me without judgement and without prejudice. They knew there was nothing they could do. They had to let it play out. I would drive back to Somerset when I could. This would result in accusations from That Person about me 'running back to my ex'. I would see my dog; I would see my friend. Then I would go back and let it all be around me again. I was living in the same fog that I'd lived in when I was in London. I was totally fucking myself up. But I so badly wanted it all to work out, and I was still being told it would work itself out. Two months in, I still didn't have any internet. I had lost count of the number of times That Person said we would do something and had then cancelled at the last minute. There had been no date.

Just before Christmas 2020, That Person had agreed with their partner to stop all contact with me. That Person's partner knew we were friends, and had suspected for some time it was more than that. That Person's partner had had enough. That Person had agreed not to see me or speak to me for three months, until March, when they 'moved into their own flat'. I was inconsolable. But I went along with it. I promised not to contact them. I would do *anything* to make it work.

The day after Christmas I got a message from them saying, 'This is the last Christmas I will ever spend without you.' They would break their own rules every time.

I've been back through every single bit of communication we had around that time (and afterwards) to try to piece together how I ended up letting this get to the point that it did in June 2021. The point where I wanted to die. It's horrifying, confusing and extremely traumatising. My memory of it is fogged by immense depression and alcohol, but the facts are there in email upon email, text upon text.

It's finger-pointing, blame-setting horror, laid out for me to look at whenever I want. I kept *everything* to prove I wasn't mad, because in the aftermath of all this, That Person tried to make me feel like I was. I want to say it was all my fault. And a lot of it was. I should never, ever have got into that situation. I am ashamed and embarrassed about it, and I think I've made that quite clear. But I am not and never was mad.

I would go into spirals. I have always been really honest about my mental health on social media, but I was told not to be by That Person because their partner was watching my posts. At one point That Person told me to 'tone it down' with the posts that talked about my increasingly poor mental health and suicidal ideation because they made me look like a liability, and what would people think? They told me that it wasn't 'socially acceptable' to say those things. Still that flag wasn't red enough or apparent enough for me to shove it up their arse.

My work was suffering in an enormous way. I couldn't focus on anything. I wasn't hitting targets. I felt constantly anxious, distracted and scared. People knew. I felt like everyone knew. I was drinking more and more and more. In the time I lived in that house I probably cooked less than ten meals. I didn't need to eat any more. I survived off crisps and garage sandwiches. Back on the old Winehouse diet. I once drove my car to the garage after two bottles of wine – to find *more* wine. I am appalled that I did this. But at the time I didn't care. I didn't care about anything apart from the fact that my heart felt like it was breaking and I absolutely didn't know what to do. I just wanted it all to end.

One night in April 2021, I walked up the road, drunk, and stood on the bridge near my house that crossed the A63. The plan was to throw myself into the path of the lorries below, but there was a police car parked to the right of the bridge and not enough trucks to make it an absolute. So I bottled it and went home. I felt nothing but shame that I couldn't even get that right.

I'd felt like this before – or I'd felt very similar before. Of course I had. Panama, London, the whole of my twenties. But then there had always been support, and there had almost always been a finite end.

Now there wasn't. I didn't have the tools, I didn't have the support, I didn't have my family, I didn't have my friends, I couldn't go out and I didn't have fucking internet connection – which doesn't sound like a big deal until you're alone in a pandemic with no way of contacting your support network or watching cat videos. Because I couldn't see an end, it looked like the only way forward was to end it myself.

In June 2021, I was sent away on a foreign trip. It was the first time I had been abroad since I'd moved. I should never have gone, but I wanted to prove I was alright. I didn't ask for help, I thought I'd lose my job. I thought once I was there it would sort itself out. The situation on that trip was intolerable, and my behaviour totally went against work rules. I tried to hide it from everyone. I tried being funny and cool. I was a mess. Everyone knew I was a fucking mess, but everyone sort of went along with it. I was properly panicking now. Despite all this, despite the shell of a person I had become, I managed to physically get across that country on foot. To a point I still managed to get the job done. Unbelievable.

That Person drove me back from the airport after that trip. They stood in my kitchen and said, 'I love you. It's all going to be OK.'

That was the last time I ever spoke to them.

When they left, I drank a bottle and a half of wine then phoned my boss to lie about how well the trip had gone. Then I decided to kill myself. The pain inside me was just too immense. I put on my running kit; I was going to run to the bridge. Then I lay down on the sofa and cried. When I woke up it was super late. Something told me to go to someone. I called my friend Sarah and asked where she was watching the football (it was cup final night) and drove (over the limit) to her house with a bottle of wine in one hand and another one hidden in my overnight bag. I sat in the pub and watched football. I felt nothing and spoke to nobody. I think at some point I told her I wanted to die. I don't remember if it was at the pub or at her house. She made me promise to go straight into work the next day and ask for help. So I did. I drove to work the next day trying not to look at the central reservation, trying not to drive into it, walked into the office, started to cry and told my manager I couldn't do it any more. I told them I needed help. And I got it.

I went numb and everything happened very quickly. Phone calls. Whispers. Me just trying to breathe through horrible sobs. I was driven back to my house where I packed a small bag. I was then driven back to Somerset – 250 miles away – by my manager. They wouldn't allow me to drive my own car. That was left at work. More phone calls were made on the way, a support network was being formed, a crisis team was coming together. My mum, Julius, the NHS helpline. My manager bought food along the way; I refused to eat any of it. I just sat there crying and trying to explain to them and other people on the phone what the fuck was going on. And apologising *a lot*.

I messaged That Person and said that I was unwell and was being driven home. They messaged back and told me (and this is word for word): 'I'm so sorry but I don't think I can emotionally support you any more. Despite everything that's happened, you will always be my best friend.'

You will always be my best friend. You can fuck off, mate.

I just felt nothing.

When I got back to Somerset the door opened and Julius was there looking really worried. I don't even think I was crying at this point. I think I just stood there. I do remember looking at Pickle and feeling absolutely nothing. NOTHING. I felt nothing at all for her beautiful face, her waggy body and the love she emitted, so pleased Mummy was home.

My manager left, I went to the shop, bought two bottles of wine and drank them. I cried and cried and cried.

This felt like the shattering of everything, and this was my rock bottom.

The shame, the abandonment, the embarrassment, the broken promises, the exhaustion from pretending, the feeling I had totally lost myself. The relief, the gratitude, the vulnerability, the feeling it had very almost been the end. The nagging feeling that I still wanted it to be the end. I finished both bottles, and just like that the drinking was over. That was the last time I ever drank alcohol.

I slept for days – maybe two or three days – in that little spare bedroom in Shepton Mallet. I deleted all social media from my phone and switched it off. I didn't want anyone to find me. Julius was in touch with both my mum and my work. I woke up only to eat or drink and then I went back to sleep again. I didn't leave the house. I would wake up and find Julius sitting on the bed next to me, and sometimes Pickle's soft little nose nudging me. Sometimes she slept on the bed, her hot little body next to me. Soft ears. The sound of her breathing. Big sighs. Unconditional love. I still felt nothing. It was like my brain and thoughts were on pause. Literally nothing. No worries, no sadness. Nothing. The only thought I had appeared factual – a holding screen, a buffering thought. *I can NEVER feel like this again*. It ticker-taped through my brain: *I can NEVER feel like this again, I can NEVER feel like this again, I can NEVER feel like this again*. There was no fixing this, no putting a plaster on it, no hack and no quick fix. This was the end. Of what, I didn't know, but this had to be the end.

PART THREE
THE REALISINGS

Aaaaand breathe out.

It took me nine weeks to recover from that day enough to be able to write the blog that would blow the doors off my life as I knew it. Nine fucking weeks. What follows is an excerpt. The full thing is available on my website. When I wrote this blog, I knew it would signal a sort of freedom for me. I didn't know how much of a freedom that would turn out to be.

BLOG EXCERPT: I WANTED TO BE INVISIBLE; AT MY LOWEST I JUST WANTED TO BE DEAD

Published 16 September 2021
Age: 40
Time sober: 2 months, 2 days
Years running: 13
Listen to: 'Everything I Wanted' – Billie Eilish

Ten weeks ago, I reached my rock bottom. Some people call it a 'shattering' and that's what it felt like. It had been years and years in the making, but previously I had patched myself up and glued myself together more times than I can remember, to keep functioning while the storm roared and roared in my head, occasionally just dropping to a slight wind before ultimately picking up again. There were ups, there were downs. Everyone has them. When I was good, I was super fucking good. Everyone wants a piece of Allie when she's on top form because she's fucking brilliant. Everyone wants the best bits. Turns out very, very few people want a piece of her when she's not. To all the people that say there is no longer a stigma around mental health, I say fuck off. There is a huge stigma around it. It's fucking massive. Most of you, sitting here, reading this, are frightened of people who say they want to kill themselves. Terrified of them. You don't know what to say, you don't know what to do, so you back off and pretend it's not happening. That is a fact. The thought that someone might want to do that to themselves scares the shit out of you. The irony is nobody, not one person, could ever be more scared of me than I was of myself on that day.

I have ALWAYS been someone that has battled against myself; it's not like I've ever hidden it (despite being told to do so by a number of people because apparently it's 'not socially acceptable'). I've documented it publicly for both myself and for other people in my blogs, interviews, on Instagram, Facebook, all the good places. I've had some good times where I've really felt like maybe I was rid of the whole thing, I've had some times where there have been wobbles and I have managed to avert disaster (or so I thought), and I have had some times where I have just felt so shit that I've not told the whole truth and tried to mask over it because even I am sick of talking about it. I am ashamed of that. I am ashamed of covering it up. Sometimes I feel like a broken record, but maybe writing about it helps others to know they are not alone. It certainly helps me to write it down.

A lot of you who follow me on socials will know that I pride myself on how 'incredibly honest' I am all the time. Well, even I am not that honest. Example in point. A lot of you will also have seen my lovely trip away for work a couple of months ago. I looked like I was having a fucking great time, right? Go back and have a look at those posts. Back out after a year of cancelled trips, doing what I do best in one of the most beautiful places on earth – how could I not be happy? Well, guess what? That was actually one of the most difficult and frightening weeks of my life. I literally could not trust myself. I put on a good (ish) show, but inside me lava was running through my veins, there was a constant bin fire in my head, and I was completely emotionally fucked. I should not have gone on that trip. I should have asked for help sooner. I hid how ill I was from my employer, and for that I am truly sorry. I thought I could manage myself. I absolutely could not. I was dying. Or at least planning on dying. And I felt like there was nothing I could do about it.

Although I shouldn't be, I am super embarrassed about admitting all this, here on paper, especially as a lot of people see me as a very strong, resilient human being. I feel like it makes me look weak. In reality, admitting it makes me strong and goes partway to getting over it for good. I also think it's important to really try to be honest now. Over the course of almost a year I have been beaten down emotionally, mentally and psychologically by my environment and circumstances, by some of the people I have chosen to have in my life, and by myself. I was drowning. My gradual descent into madness was even caught on camera recently. Anyone that watched the SDW100 video The Running Channel made [bit.ly/SDW100] and saw me have a proper meltdown when my pacer ran on ahead with someone else – that is my abandonment being triggered. It was not her fault. It appears completely irrational. In my head it was completely sane. It makes me look like a whiny little bitch. It makes me utterly hate myself. I am cringing even writing this. But that's what these mental health issues can do to an apparently 'resilient' person. It. Can. Happen. To. Anyone. If you ignore it, it will not go away.

This all makes me sound really fucking needy, and I honestly feel so, so embarrassed about writing it all down. You do get needy when you are completely isolated, super fucking depressed and your worst fears are coming true. But the interesting thing is, as much as you are needy – for affection, for truth, for approval and for comfort – you also start to shut down socially and live in your own head. You actually don't trust or believe anyone at all, which is highly ironic as the people that love you are telling you that you're great. But people can tell you they love you or that you're awesome until they're blue in the face. They can give you a fucking crown. It's too late. You just don't believe them. The hatred you feel for yourself, the repeated battering you have had, the pain, is so chronic that nothing can get through it. If the same things happen over and over again, you can never imagine a time when they won't. You don't trust people, you don't trust situations and, worst of all, you don't trust yourself.

Sometimes I feel these triggers as a physical pain that rages through me in waves. It's not something I can explain in words that well, as much as I try. It just makes me fucking hate myself and feel utterly, utterly sick. And feeling like that only proves all the worst thoughts I have about myself: that I am not good enough, that I am worthless, that I am a fraud, that I am a piece of fucking shit and that I deserve to be miserable or, even better, dead. It is utter torture. I have lived with this on and off for almost twenty-five years. I cannot and will not live with it any longer. I am accepting I am far from perfect. I have fucked up more times than I can count, I am damaged and traumatised, but I am alive, and with love, support and time I can improve. The world is mine. And I am going to try my best to take it.

CHAPTER 7
TAKE THE PIECES AND BUILD THEM SKYWARDS

Listen to: 'Machines' – Biffy Clyro

There's a Biffy Clyro song I fucking love. It's called 'Machines'. Singer Simon Neil wrote it about his mother passing away. It's a song that talks about falling apart. It's aching in its pain, but visceral in its optimism. The most important lyric to me is that one about taking the pieces and building them skywards. I have those words tattooed on my right shoulder. You can't just come out of something like this a new person. You can't just completely change. You have to take the pieces off the floor and slowly rebuild them. And that takes ages. And never really stops.

Nine weeks is a long time. And that's how long it took to get me from the bottom of the barrel to standing on my own two feet again, albeit with many people holding my hands and waiting for me to fall. In that time, I avoided all social media, almost all outside world contact and all alcohol. I was like a toddler. I ate. I slept. I didn't really exercise for the first few weeks, or leave whichever house I was in under guard. I didn't listen to music or read the news. I lived between my mum's and Julius's, pretty much under adult supervision. During the second week, I went to my mum's, and she tried her best to get me some NHS help, but it wasn't happening. The waiting lists were too long, and the general practitioner (GP) was too fucking general. When my mum took me to her local GP and attempted to explain the situation, I was met with the classic head nod and 'sorry you're experiencing low mood, there's a huge waiting list for therapy so have some drugs' chat. The GP then asked me what I wanted to do right there in that moment. I told her I wanted to fucking die, got up and left. My mum started crying. I am so sorry, Mum. But I did. I just wanted to die. That feeling didn't leave me for weeks. I wanted someone to understand. Nobody understood.

I remember screaming at crisis workers on phone lines, at the insurance company who wouldn't pay for private help (pre-existing condition) and my own mother when she tried to help me. One day I scratched the skin off my own face with my fingernails in rage. My mum had to call my brother and get him to take me away from the house. He took me to the beach and calmed me down. It was fucking dark. Dark but necessary.

During that time, nobody told me or suggested to me that I was an alcoholic or that I should stop drinking. I did. I told myself and I accepted it. A few weeks before the breakdown, when I was away, I'd been reading a book by Bryony Gordon. That book was *Glorious Rock Bottom*. I'd read a few of Bryony's books, and I liked her a lot. She was recently sober, and this was how she got to be that way. I don't know why I chose that book; sometimes I would read books about really fucked-up people to prove to myself I wasn't as fucked up as them and everyone was like this. I think now I read those books looking for some kind of quick fix to get out of it. Whatever the reason, this book was different. I remember feeling an absolute affinity with her while I was reading it, stuck outside a COVID testing centre in the Eastern Caribbean with a hangover and depression so bad that the only thing getting me through was drinking more. I remember thinking, *Fucking hell, this is a bit close to home. Maybe I should stop drinking.* Then my name was called, and I shut the book and went into the testing centre and forgot about it. There were so many echoes of my life in that book. Still I did nothing. Is that what you are doing now, reader? Are you doing nothing?

It's important to point out that while alcohol didn't necessarily cause my problems, it didn't help my decision-making process, my depression, my recognition of what was going on or my acceptance of the fact that I was not dealing with, and had never dealt with, the underlying issues. I masked it all with booze. I used it as a temporary measure – a quick fix, a numbing agent – until it wasn't temporary or quick any more, it was permanent and took a while to work.

The first few weeks sober were hellish – of course they were. I am an addict. Always will be. But I was desperate to feel better, and I would have done anything. ANYTHING. I got dry on my own, cold-turkey style. I think everyone around me thought it was a phase – a good phase, but a phase. I somehow linked the alcohol to that searing, burning, roaring pain, self-hatred and constant suicidal ideation I'd felt for the last few months and, hey presto: I didn't want to do it any more. It was not and is not easy. It's a battle I face every day and will until I die. I know I am an alcoholic. And I know that if I slip (and there have already been times when it's been touch and go) all hell will break loose. My sobriety is my number one priority. I guard it closely, like you would a baby. Because that is what it is, a little baby that needs to be protected. I need to grow and nurture it, and anyone or anything that threatens that has absolutely no place in my life.

In those nine weeks I started doing things that made me feel calm and in control. I had to. They included, but weren't limited to, jigsaw puzzles, crosswords, ironing and, bizarrely, re-upholstering chairs. Like the races and events I used to block book, these things had a start, a middle and an end and were enough of a challenge that I felt like I was alive. After a few weeks, I started running again – just a little bit, but I started. When you literally don't know who you are any more, that can be a difficult thing to do. I took all my races and events out of the diary. I cleared it all. Nothing to see here. I got out when I could, and I tried to be grateful. I felt like I'd fucked running as well as everything else because I'd just not been doing it as much, and when I was doing it, I wasn't present. I tried to be gentle with running. It was little and not very often at that point. For the first time in my adult life, I put myself above everything else and actually looked after myself. I listened to what my body was telling me and responded. It was easy because I had to. I had run out of options. It was do or die. 'Do the basics well' became my mantra. Eat, sleep, drink water, journal.

And Pickle. Oh, Pickle. She knew. She just knew. After a few days of sleeping, feelings started coming back, and that in itself was traumatic. You know the old adage: the best thing about sobriety is you get your feelings back, the worst thing is ... you get your feelings back. Yep. And I felt so guilty. So fucking guilty I had put my work and perceived happiness above her. Yet here she was, night after night, day after day, just lying there, looking after me, cuddling me, letting me cry into her super-fluffy neck, licking tears off my face, making funny little noises and telling me without speaking that she loved me just as I was. In the first few days I felt like a new bond was formed between us. One that was absolutely unbreakable. One that said, 'It's OK, Mummy, you're home and you're safe and I love you.' I will never, ever leave her again. I made her that promise then and I'll keep it until the day one of us dies.

Work had offered to help me out with some counselling sessions, and that was a game changer. Throughout my life, I'd tried every single bit of counselling in the book and stuck with none of them, but my mum had mentioned one of her friends (a psychiatrist) recommended looking at ACT – Acceptance and Commitment Therapy. She also recommended a book called *The Happiness Trap* by Russ Harris. I took one look at the cover and thought, *Fuck that shit*, but then remembered I wanted to die and would do anything to not feel that way, so reserved judgement and started reading it. I read it cover to cover in about two days and still think it's one of the greatest books ever written.

ACT works on the premise that we should stop avoiding, denying and struggling with our emotions, thoughts and feelings and learn to not only accept them but to commit to actions and behaviour to improve our well-being. I had literally been avoiding, denying and struggling with every thought I had had for the last twenty-five years. The thought of accepting that shit made me feel sick. It made me feel like I was backing down or accepting I was broken and sad and always would be. But acceptance doesn't mean accepting that everything is awful forever. It means accepting that you are having these thoughts, feelings and emotions, not trying to change them or get rid of them, but trying to understand them and seeing them more helpfully. It's then that you can start responding to them rather than reacting. It's only through acceptance that you can start getting better at anything. It's the single greatest lesson I learnt during this whole process. Acceptance is incredibly difficult but ultimately a superpower.

Back to the counselling. All therapists carry out an initial assessment prior to treatment. They then send you an overview on diagnosis (moderate anxiety, severe depression, potential PTSD in my case) and treatment plan. Here's part of the letter that was sent to me after that assessment back in July 2021.

> Listening to your story, I was struck by how your trust in others was repeatedly broken by the way people who were close to you behaved. It's not surprising that these experiences continue to affect you in your life today, particularly when they are so strongly at odds with your values. At the same time, it was heartening to hear how you have repeatedly found strength and resilience to overcome very difficult periods in your life, and over time move away from harmful environments or relationships. You've also recently found important motivation and commitment to change some of the unhelpful patterns of behaviour you experience. With your commitment to no longer use alcohol, you've also already made an important and impressive step towards allowing space for difficult feelings, rather than avoiding them and pushing back.
>
> You've clearly reflected on how past experiences have affected you and continue to affect you in your life now. You identified the need to make changes, and importantly to understand how your difficulties are maintained. You described your 'need for approval' as an ongoing difficulty which recurrently affects your mood and your sense of self-worth. You also described having identified core values: honesty, integrity and kindness. Perhaps you are also seeking to apply these values to yourself more at this point in your life?

'Perhaps you are also seeking to apply these values to yourself more at this point in your life.' That last sentence. That floored me.

Values. Apparently, they're a thing.

I'd never really thought about values until I read *The Happiness Trap* prior to sorting out a therapist. I'd never thought what mine were. I'm not sure if people do on a day-to-day basis.

Values are loosely defined as principles or behaviours that you decide are ultimately important in your life. The book recommended I started with my values; that I worked out what these were prior to continuing with treatment and recovery.

The second I sat down to think about this exercise, I realised I'd only ever thought about other people's value judgements of me – how much *they* thought I was worth or what *they* thought I was about. I had never considered my own value or values. Of course, I knew right from wrong, and I knew what was good and what was bad behaviour, but I wasn't clear about what I wanted to see in my own behaviour or that of others. It was a massive hole in my psyche. It didn't take long for me to come up with a list of three. Three things that I wanted to be seen as. Three values that I wanted to live my life by. Three values I wanted to have as non-negotiables. They were honesty, kindness and integrity.

Now having read this book to this point, I am sure you can see the issue here. There is no fucking way I was living, or had been living, in line with any of those values.

I hadn't been honest with myself, my family, my friends or employers about anything. Not about how ill I was, not about how sad I was, not about how much I was drinking, not about anything. I'd lied to people left, right and centre for a really long time.

I'd not been particularly kind to people either. I had an eighteen-month relationship with someone who was married, for fuck's sake. I was known for my acerbic wit and legendary put-downs; most of them were pretty unkind. Funny, but unkind. Generally, when I loved or cared about someone, I displayed kindness, and I was always kind to animals, but I had a quick temper and was absolutely not kind to myself or people that pissed me off.

And integrity. Where had that come from? I had spent years

pretending to be something that I wasn't in all walks of life. I often told people, 'What you see is what you get', but that wasn't true either. What you got was me trying to hide what you *actually* got. Because if you actually saw what was going on, you sure as shit wouldn't want it. Again, I wasn't being honest. I was severely lacking integrity.

But these were the three words I gravitated towards; these were the three things that I wanted to be. They were the values I held highest in other people – which is incredible when you look at my history, with men especially. I might have *wanted* people to display these values, but I didn't get that back or give it back at all. I allowed people to act like pricks because at the time, those values were negotiable; everything was negotiable as long as I felt wanted. They were a 'nice to have' not an 'absolutely must have'. After reading that book and talking to my new therapist, I decided to make them non-negotiable, both in my behaviour and the behaviour of others; it's a lot easier said than done.

Nowadays I try to signpost everything back to those three words. Everything I do, say, write, work on, the people I work with, the projects I take part in, the things I buy – I keep those three words in mind. All decisions lead back to them. They are now absolutely non-negotiable. I still sometimes make mistakes and find myself saying or doing something that isn't kind, or ordering something off Amazon that I am not entirely sure isn't made in a sweatshop, but when I do those things, I catch myself, question myself and am kind to myself; nobody is perfect – aim for progression, not perfection. Living according to my values has made my life so much simpler and more streamlined. Decisions pretty much make themselves. You have to be constantly on watch, though. This stuff doesn't just happen overnight. And this rebuild was far from over. Far, far from over.

Part of the picking up the pieces/rebuilding thing involved sifting through the bits that were just not helpful and getting rid of them. There were things I desperately wanted to keep in my life and was terrified to even consider throwing away. The drinking was one of those things. My job was another.

For so long I had held on to this limiting belief that I was a better version of myself when I'd had a drink. People say it all the time, don't they? That they're more relaxed, more fun, more carefree, sexier. But that's not true. It's a story that we tell ourselves because it has been hammered into us as fact – by society, by advertisers, by birthday cards, by 'funny' chalk signs outside pubs. We are conditioned to drink alcohol as if it is the most normal thing in the world. In fact, you're seen as odd if you don't do it. If you're not drinking alcohol at a social function, people ask you *why* you're not drinking it. They never ask *why you are* drinking it, do they? This is literally the *only* time we do this. You don't ask someone why they don't want ketchup on their chips, why they're not wearing a hat, or why they don't eat apples, so why do we ask people why they don't want any alcohol in their drink? Fucking weird.

Hitting that rock bottom may well have been the best thing that could have happened to me because it really wasn't a choice to not drink. I honestly don't feel like I have a choice. It's don't drink or death for me. But that didn't make stopping easy. It's one day at a time, and in a society that tells you to ingest an addictive poison at every available opportunity – weddings, funerals, births, deaths, football, cricket, Fridays, Saturdays, Sunday mornings, all the fucking time – it's not easy. 'Here, have some of this highly addictive poison, but don't get addicted to it! Oh, and if you *do* get addicted, it's your fault, not ours.' The way the drinks industry works, and is allowed to work, is absolutely fucked. But that might be for another book. For now, for me, the drinking was in the bin. The job, on the other hand, was another problem altogether.

I could not wait to get back to work and was pushing the envelope on that quite hard. My boss came to see me a few times while I was recovering, and while they showed kindness and concern, they did not mince their words when it came to telling me I had properly fucked up. I would no longer be trusted to go out on trips. My rehabilitation into work was going to be a long and slow one, and I had to accept that this was down to me and my behaviour alone. As painful and embarrassing as this was, I did just that. I tried to be kind to myself and put it down as a lesson, rather than me being a fuck-up. It was yet another reason why I should never drink again. I don't think my boss believed I would never drink again. I don't think anyone did.

My return to work was pushed back by another few weeks and I felt distraught. I just wanted to get on with things. But I needed to take my time. As the weeks passed, I started to get my ducks in a row. I wanted to move back up north, but not to that flat where all this had happened. I never wanted to go back there again. I wanted to move back to show that I wouldn't be chased away from somewhere by fear. Looking back I find this very odd behaviour, but I did it. I started looking online at other places to live near where Julius was planning to move. His son was due to go to secondary school and he too was moving north. I thought if I lived within a few miles of him, it would make life easier for both of us with shared dog care and a bit of support. I found a house to rent about forty-five minutes away from my old place and made an offer without even going to see it. It was in a tiny village and looked perfect – much bigger with lots of windows and a conservatory upstairs – plus the landlord would allow me to bring Pickle. I was overjoyed when they called and said I could move in a few weeks later. I was going home. I went back to the old flat and packed at record speed, spending one last night there before handing over the keys and vowing to never, ever go back there again. I'm so dramatic.

I helped Julius move and he helped me. My house was three miles from his. Perfect. We had support, but we could keep our distance. When I moved in, I redecorated the whole place. I made it a home, and I went back to work. It was weird going back. I felt like everyone was looking at me like I was a nutcase. I'd asked my boss to ask them not to talk to me about it – to carry on as normal. But that was impossible. The last time they'd seen me I was a fucking mess. I felt isolated and paranoid from the minute I got back into the office. I felt like they all thought I might suddenly walk in one day with a concealed weapon, open fire and kill everyone. It was really difficult maintaining the professional boundary when both my boss, my manager and most of the staff had seen me at my lowest, lowest ebb.

I am not going to go into what happened over the weeks that followed my return to work, because I can't. But it was chaotic, totally unexpected and for me extremely painful. Throughout it all, I did not drink. I eventually parted ways with the events company and for the second time in my life, I was in a new flat, jobless, with low to no income. But this time it was different. I was sober.

I didn't know what the fuck I was going to do, and it was scary. But I *was* still sober. And I'd started to notice things changing in me. I was a lot calmer. Like, super calm. My anxiety had all but gone; even though financially I was in a really shitty situation I just wasn't worried. *I'll get a job at Amazon,* I thought. I was grateful a lot of the time. For a lot of stuff. I had started noticing my feelings were dictated by my thoughts and not vice versa. I knew how to choose helpful thoughts over unhelpful ones now. I was winning the battle with my brain more often than not.

And Pickle. My girl, my light, the love of my life. Every day a reason to get up and go out. Someone to talk to, someone to cuddle, someone to watch shit TV with. She made me laugh every day without fail. The apple of my eye. Unconditional love pouring out of her. I was running again and enjoying it – proper running, forty to fifty miles a week with Pickle. I had started putting a little calendar together for the next year – a list of races I wanted to do. I had written reminders of how to live life like a normal person and stuck them around the house in places where I would see them. I lived by those reminders. I still do.

On my bathroom mirror is a note saying, 'Eyes (contacts), wash face, clean teeth – be fucking grateful always.' This is there because I hadn't done any of those things as a routine for years. I didn't think it was worthwhile cleaning my teeth or washing my face most of the time. My contacts stayed in until they fell out.

On my fridge is a note that says, 'Do the basics well – eat three meals a day, drink two litres of water, sleep eight to ten hours.' At the start that is all I had to do, and even now if I can get that done, I can get other stuff done, right? I'm accountable to a Post-it.

And in my bedroom, there are three notes on the mirror that read, 'Do not question your decisions', 'Your past has zero effect in your future' and 'You are allowed to rest'. Because all those things are true, and they help me stay on track.

I was creating a little world in this new house. A world for myself and Pie. The anger at the loss of my dream job dissipated when I thought about what I *did* have. My Pie, my sanity, my sobriety, my mental health, even my running. Surely those things were worth more than any job? I started to believe that they were. I believe they are. I was creating a new story in that house. It wasn't easy – some days were excruciating – writing a new story, and getting your brain to believe it, takes time. But I was brave enough to start writing it. I was taking the pieces and building them skywards.

All this is very lovely, isn't it? But I still needed to earn money. I had a little bit trickling in from here and there, various little freelance projects, but I didn't have anything concrete and I didn't know where I was going to find a job I liked or could actually do. I'm not sure where you go from being a professional adventurer; there's not really a section for that on most job search websites.

It all came back to those values – everything did. When I looked at them in a desperate attempt to work out what the fuck I was going to do for money, what jumped out at me was this idea that I liked helping people, and that ticked the values box. I'd loved it in my previous job – getting people across mountains, deserts and jungles; seeing them achieve more than they thought possible. That was my jam. I was well into it. So how could I do that in real life without a company paying me to do it? I decided to start coaching.

Every now and again, someone would ask me about coaching and I would laugh at them. I wasn't a coach. I was just a runner – and not a very good one at that. I had no qualifications and had never coached anyone in my life. But people *had* asked me. Maybe it was an option. I wondered what would happen if I put it out into the universe – the fact I was looking to do a bit of an experiment and take on some coaching clients. So I did. And within one week of asking on Instagram if anyone fancied being coached by me, I had ten clients. Within a month I had fifteen. And just like that, I was an ultrarunning and endurance coach. And it was fucking brilliant.

At the time of writing, two years after I started that business, I still have five of those clients – and a whole load more. The business has gone from strength to strength, offering not just one-to-one coaching but group sessions and multi-day workshops that sell out as soon as they go up on the website. I am my own boss, I do what I like, I work when I want and I only work with people that I like, respect and can learn from.

But, most importantly, I am working in line with those values. I am helping people to achieve incredible things through honesty, integrity and, for the most part, kindness (I am an arsehole to them sometimes ...).

I am not like other coaches. I do it my way. I work on people's brains just as much as I work on their running plans. I am not a therapist, or a psychologist, or an anything-ist. I have my own lived experience to work with and that's it, but that seems to be working really well. It's a massive gift to be able to use my powers for good. Could I have achieved this if I was still drinking? Could I fuck.

CHAPTER 8
MIND THE GAP, PLEASE

Listen to: 'Calgary' – Bon Iver

I talk to my coaching clients about the knowing–doing gap all the time. There's knowing something – and then there's putting it into action. Most people fail on the second bit. The knowing–doing gap is a term that I first heard used in Brad Stulberg's epic *The Practice of Groundedness* – a book that I'll talk about in the next chapter because it's just so fucking good. You'll also find it in loads of other books, TED talks and YouTube videos covering everything from corporate management to dealing with angry teenagers. The knowing–doing gap refers to the disconnect between knowing something, and doing it.

I find it really helpful to actually see the gap as just that – a gap. It helps me know when I'm doing it. How many times have you heard someone say, 'Do as I say not as I do', or, 'I'm really good at giving advice to other people but awful at following it myself'? They're shouting that shit from the bottom of the crevasse that separates knowing and doing. They've fallen down the gap. Knowing alone is not enough. You have to put that knowledge into action. And that takes practice – loads of it.

Way back when I started running, and while I was ill, I was using running as a way to not feel depressed for a few hours. I was running away from the person I was, as opposed to running towards the person I wanted to be. That was literally it. Running also had very little to do with my recovery from that breakdown. It does, however, have everything to do with my long-term health, happiness and purpose going forward, and it is also the number one way I learnt how to bridge the knowing–doing gap. I still use running to test the stuff I learnt in therapy, from reading and from hours sitting in my living room or at my desk thinking, *How can I do life differently?* Running is now a safe space for me to test the good stuff in; it might be the same for you. And it doesn't have to be running; it can be anything you want to get your teeth into. Get on a bike if you absolutely have to, but don't expect us to be friends.

I felt like rock bottom had stripped a lot of stuff away from me. I felt a bit like I had a new opportunity – a clean slate to work on. The shame had for the most part gone. Everyone knew everything now, and the world hadn't exploded. I had an opportunity to do things differently, and I was totally committed to doing that because of that 'I can never feel like this again' ticker-tape day.

Historically, running had bought me time to process my shitty thoughts, but it had also shown me on a few occasions that my thoughts alone couldn't kill me or even stop me from doing hard things. I had managed to get through every bad thought I'd ever had, and I had never not finished a race. But I had also never run a race as a totally sober person. I had never run a race feeling every single emotion and having to deal with it without being hungover, depressed, slightly drunk or knowing there was a drink at the end to shut it up. That was brand new territory for me.

My mini practice sessions on how to apply 'getting through fucking shit thoughts' as a drinker were pretty huge – Mongolia, Namibia, Panama, 100-mile races, multi-day epics – but I'd had none as a sober person. Running let me have those feelings on the move, and it let me prove them wrong while I was thinking about them – but they would always end in the pub. They would never fully be dealt with. They would be drunk away.

And running is running. Running is not life. It has a start, a middle and an end. Life does and it doesn't. You know you're not at the start of life, but none of us know where the middle or the end will be. For me, that's what made sitting with thoughts and feelings outside of running so hard. I didn't know when the thoughts were going to end. I thought if they didn't end, I would die of them. I didn't know I had power and choice over them. At the end of my running events or training runs, everything I had thought about or felt went back in the cupboard the minute I had a drink – the same cupboard I keep my poles, bags and snacks in – and I 'felt better'. For about twenty minutes. In life, it isn't like that.

In early sobriety, I spent a lot of time asking myself how I could do those ridiculous events time after time, sometimes week after week, and finish all of them, even when I was depressed, tired and for the most part hungover, but not apply the same mindset to my life. And I eventually worked it out. While running was at times absolutely helping me sort through the shit in my brain while I was doing it, it was also acting as a numbing agent in the same way that alcohol was. I was trying to numb myself to the thoughts by having them over and over again in a safe space and almost neutralising them or normalising them, as opposed to choosing to believe other thoughts that may have been more useful.

The moment I realised that's what had been happening was the moment I knew that I needed to do a ton of work not just on myself but on the way running was serving me. I had been running for all the wrong reasons.

During the early stages of my recovery, I read every book under the sun on addiction, mindset and performance psychology. I've included a list of some of them at the end of this book because they are all fucking bangers. In all honesty, I was looking for answers and hacks – quick ways to get better – but here comes a spoiler: there are no quick ways to get better. There are no hacks.

Rewiring your brain from addict to non-addict, or from performance avoidance to performance approach, or from fucking miserable to slightly more hopeful, is literally the act of learning a new language for yourself. You can't just read a French book and expect to be fluent in French (or in my case, Welsh). You can't read a book on swimming and expect to be lining up at the Olympics next to Adam

Peaty; you have to practise. And that's where I was going wrong. I wasn't doing the work.

When I was drinking, I couldn't do the work. I didn't want to, I didn't know there was work to do, and I was too pissed and depressed to even conceive of the idea that I could feel better. When I got sober, when 'I can never feel like this again' happened, I started doing the work. I was so desperate for anything at all to help me that I started doing the work. The hard work.

As well as having a good few weeks of pretty intense ACT therapy, I got myself a coach. Hazel Robertson specialises in time and mindset coaching. I started working with her first and foremost to help me sort out my shit with my newly formed coaching company, but she became invaluable to me doing the work on my new brain language because she held me accountable; I had to speak to her every week. One of the good things about the breakdown was it had made me super comfortable with asking for help. I never used to do that. I always felt like it made me look like I wasn't capable. If I can't do something now, I will ask for help straight away – and that included asking for help on rewiring my brain.

The number one thing that Hazel taught me is that I am not my thoughts. I am the thinker, but not the thoughts. It's all well and good saying that, but try believing it. She also taught me that humans have around 60,000 thoughts a day. And only one per cent of those are useful. This does not surprise me; I spend a lot of time thinking about what Pickle is thinking/doing/dreaming about or whether pigs would be the apex species if they had opposable thumbs. Hazel also taught me that I have a choice as to what I think, how I think and what I believe. A choice. Mind blown. Time to do the work.

Knowing this stuff is great. But just knowing it doesn't change anything. You have to do it. And you have to do it all the time. That is the practice, that is the work and that is how you bridge the knowing–doing gap. There's no hack, there's no quick route around it. It is tiring, sometimes frustrating, sometimes upsetting, but without sounding like a total meme, it gets results. But it took practice. And how did I practise? I took the knowing–doing gap for a couple of runs.

During my illness, I cancelled all my races, but as I started to feel better, things started cropping up that I liked the look of. Everything I wanted to do was either horrible or hard or both. The first fun-times jog to draw me in was the Arc of Attrition. The Arc is a 100-mile foot race held on the last weekend of January. It starts in Coverack on the south coast of Cornwall and follows the South West Coast Path all the way to Porthtowan on the north coast. The race starts at 12 p.m., and is run almost entirely in darkness on some of the most difficult and feared sections of trail running that England has to offer. With 14,000 feet of elevation, clifftop sections that offer extreme exposure to wind, rain and hail above, bone-crushing rocks below and almost guaranteed shit weather, it's no wonder the DNF rate for this race is so high – usually hovering around sixty per cent. *I love Cornwall*, I thought. *I'm in.* I think I was also looking for something that would absolutely make me feel more shit physically than I could make myself feel mentally. Another part of me wanted to prove something to all the people that I felt had 'wronged' me that I was 'better' – ridiculous, I know. And another part of me wanted to use it as a 'test' to see if I was better – if the work I had done with my therapist and on myself had, erm ... worked. Again, ridiculous, I know. I entered. I was going to do it.

Then there was the Dragon's Back Race (DBR) pencilled in for September 2022. Six days running the length of Wales with extremely tight cut-off times each day and logistical hurdles: a weight limit for what you could take with you, no crews or pacers, self-navigation, more potentially shit weather, camping overnight with people I didn't know, early starts, late finishes and the small matter of over 11,000 feet of ascent on most of the days. I'd been offered a place at this race the year before but deferred it due to not being able to give it the training it deserved. My then boss had also strongly suggested that it wasn't cool to be out promoting another race company when I worked for him. Now I was a free agent, I could do what the fuck I liked. I entered. And then there was my Land's End to John o'Groats spectacular to think about.

When I'd stopped working for the events company there was one thing that I didn't want them to take from me: my one and only opportunity to run the length of the UK. They agreed I could still go and do this route with the six other people I'd signed up, and that was a relief. I'd been instrumental in coming up with the early plan and logistics for this event. Thirty-five days' running over 1,000 miles from Land's End to John o'Groats on some of the best trails the UK has to offer. This wasn't the normal LEJOG route, and having been scuppered by COVID on two occasions, it was now planned for June 2022. Back in September 2021, I had spent three weeks recceing parts of the route. On occasion, That Person had been there. For the most part, that trip had been shrouded in arguments, secrecy and lies. Three weeks trying to pretend this relationship was going the way I wanted it to. I wanted to go and reclaim the route as mine, I wanted to go and make new memories in places that harboured terrible ones. I wanted to be among the first people to complete this route. After my sobriety, getting this done was my priority above all else.

So, three huge events in one year, a fledgling coaching business to look after and my own ongoing recovery to think about. When I planned all this, I was still in the very early stages of recovery from both addiction and mental health crisis, so I was still fucking insane. On paper it looks like not much has changed – still overdoing it, still setting the bar way too high for myself, still using running as a numbing agent. At the time I thought that year I would prove to myself and the world that I was magically better. What it actually did was put everything I'd started to learn about myself into practice in ways I'd never expected. What it did was show me the difference between knowing your shit and doing it.

When I stood at the start line of the Arc of Attrition in January 2022, I was six months sober. I couldn't believe it. I couldn't believe I had managed to stay clean for so long. The coaching business was really healthy, and I'd been meticulous in my planning for this event. I had recced the route, trained well and worked really hard on my mental health. I had a brilliant set of people on hand to crew me: Lorna, Julius and of course Pickle in her role as chief medical and cuddles officer. I'd got my new routines down: eating three meals a day, washing my face, cleaning my teeth – things that are basic to most people but had been missing from my life for a really long time.

I had settled into my new house, and while I had super-tough days where I struggled and felt like shit, I now approached the dark thoughts with love and curiosity rather than believing and fearing them. I had identified I would always live with this guy called depression and that sometimes he'd want to talk to me, and I'd have to listen. I'd identified him as that irritating lodger that lived with me permanently. I understood that even though he would sometimes talk and talk at me, I didn't have to believe what he said. I could just observe him, let it wash over me and usually go to bed. Sometimes I'd even laugh at the shit he came out with. He would be gone in the morning. It was an ongoing process, and I was trying to do a bit more work on it every day.

Don't think things were rosy – they weren't. But they were better. Sobriety suited me. But nobody's perfect, and the Arc was about to test the difference between what I knew and what I did in a way I really didn't expect.

The race started off well. I had crew meeting me every twenty miles or so, but no pacers allowed. I'd always had pacers on my 100s; I liked the company and the distraction. From the start, there was the looming thought that people didn't finish this race all the time. The announcer even said that before we set off. I told myself that that was their story, not mine, and I was going to do my best. Before the event I wrote myself a compassionate letter – something I'd read about in a number of books and something I'd learnt from my therapist. I wanted to tell myself I was ready to do my best and show myself love and respect for getting to the start line. I did it, I read it, I understood it and I packed it in my kit bag in case I needed to read it again. The full letter is on my blog, but these lines stand out:

> Nothing out there can scare you more than you scared yourself last year. No pain will be worse than that pain. These are all just old stories. You're out here creating a new one. You're a warrior. I love you.

I don't know what I expected. I don't know if I thought that my new superpowers of being kind to myself and thinking differently would come to me by magic. But they did not. It was a bastard of a race. That section of the coast path is hard – especially in January. The wet, slippery paths and rocks slow you down. Weirdly, it wasn't as nice as it had been in December when I'd visited the route for a week of glorious route recces; when the sun was shining and Pickle was there and there were no cut-offs. The pack spread out fast and I struggled being on my own with nobody to talk to. I made rookie mistakes – not eating enough and going too fast on the flat sections – and I felt *everything* was harder than it should be. I was performing from a place of fear. I knew I was. I wasn't accepting anything; I was denying it all. I was falling down the gap.

In previous races, I would have been hungover or depressed. With a filter like that firmly on, nothing else can get through. I actually think running 100-mile races hungover and depressed made them a lot easier for me. This was different. I was hyper-aware of how I felt. There was no 'come on, you piece of shit' narrative, no foggy flow to get into … it was more, 'U OK, hun?!' to myself – and, no, I was *not* OK, hun. I was worried about time and cut-offs and that meant I was not in the moment. I can't remember a lot about the first half of the race, but I know I made it to Land's End (pretty much halfway) with plenty of time to spare. And then it went to shit. My plan was to stop and eat a proper meal. I didn't do that. I stopped for less than ten minutes and had a tiny bowl of beans. It was about 2 a.m. and my crew were outside in the car park in the freezing rain and wind. I was worried about them; I wanted them to be able to get out of that car park and home as soon as possible, so I binned off my carefully thought-out plan and decided to leave and crack on ASAP so they could be comfortable. I was falling further down the gap. I *knew* this was about me and that I should be looking after myself, but I was not *doing* it. The comfortable people-pleasing tendencies that I'd displayed for so long came back, and I let them.

By the time I got to the Pendeen Watch checkpoint, I had an hour on the cut-off. I'd started being sick and doing nothing about it. That sickness came more from anxiety and trying to run that anxiety off than from a fuelling issue, although I definitely hadn't eaten enough. I now wasn't even doing the basics well. I was thinking, *Fuck, I am throwing everything up, I'm going to die,* rather than, *This is OK and is normal. Drink water, take some salt and try to get some calories in.* I'd started freaking out. I was extremely tired and hungry, and I was falling even further down the gap. At no point did I stop and try to recentre myself. While I had practised this recentring at home, I didn't believe I could do it now. I couldn't put it into practice when I needed it most. I freaked out and at mile seventy convinced myself I wasn't going to meet the cut-off at St Ives and pulled out. My first ever DNF.

I felt like absolute shit. Physically, I was done in, and at the time I couldn't put a finger on why. Spoiler: it was because I was hungry. My brain wasn't working properly because it had nothing to fuel it. I panicked. I 'knew' at Zennor that I wouldn't make the cut-off at St Ives feeling like this. Or that's what I told myself. I thought I was pacing OK, I thought that up until Land's End I had followed the plan perfectly. I absolutely hadn't.

I had believed thoughts that had very little basis in fact. And I was still doing it.

The post-event, overriding, number one thought was that this was an absolute disaster; that it proved that I was still ill and broken. I had never DNF-ed before, and I felt like it showed the world I was a fraud. I wasn't good enough. There was even a thought that maybe I *needed* to drink to be able to do this stuff – to make me hard enough. Because I was sober and had read some books and had a bit of therapy and got a coach, I thought I'd be able to manage the thoughts. But because I hadn't practised managing them enough, I couldn't. And that is how you fall down the knowing–doing gap.

It may not surprise you to know that there is yet another extremely lengthy blog about all this on my website. It took me a while before I could write it. Even though I obviously understood that I needed to be kinder to myself, I was not putting anything I had learnt into practice. It was not until a few weeks later that I had unpicked it and analysed it to the point where I was comfortable accepting that stopping was actually the kindest thing I could have done for myself in that situation. Because it was.

Old me may have pushed on. Old me may have gone on and on

until I either became a medical emergency, or timed out, or maybe even finished. But this version of me didn't. This version of me stopped. Had my sobriety made me weak? Maybe I was being *too* nice to myself? It was really confusing.

The bottom line is that I wasn't ready. Physically, I was actually OK. I was match fit and ready to go. Mentally, however, I didn't fully understand the lessons I had been teaching myself and I failed to act on old patterns of behaviour until it was too late. Previously, I'd always just cracked on regardless; the thoughts had had to get through the hangover and depression in order to register. Now, I felt and heard everything I was saying to myself. In glorious high-resolution technicolour.

It took me about a month to get over the disappointment I felt. A month! Nowadays it usually takes less than twenty-four hours. As soon as entries went live for the 2023 edition of the race, I entered. You only fail when you stop trying. I would not stop trying. In typical fashion, I turned my focus to the next big thing: running the length of the UK.

I was always looking towards the next goal regardless of what I was doing. My life was a series of what-nexts. I'd read about mindfulness, owning my energy and being in the moment – but could I do it? Fuck no. I knew that happiness/contentment/fulfilment or whatever you want to call it was not an endgame; I knew that completion of certain events or distances only gives way to more events and distances. Did I put that into action? Of course not! I just kept pushing the goalposts further and further up the road. It takes extreme hard work, time and patience, and a huge dose of self-awareness to not do that. My self-awareness was in its infancy, my patience still non-existent.

My main aim with this next project was to 'not get in the van'. The van was our support vehicle. It would be there at every checkpoint with water and snacks and to offer a lift to the injured and dying. I wanted to run the whole route and not spend any time at all in the van. I would not get in the van unless I had broken something and/or was dying. That was my golden rule. I formulated my own kill criteria – something I later found out more about reading Annie

Duke's incredible book *Quit: the Power of Knowing When to Walk Away*. I wish this book had come into my life earlier, but it actually came after my fun-times UK-long jog on recommendation from a brilliant friend. I'd urge all endurance athletes to read it. It's a belter.

Despite not reading the book, I put together my own short list of reasons that would allow me to stop and get in the van. They included: possibility of a career-ending injury (medic-backed only), inability to keep down food or water for long periods (dehydration/heatstroke/hypothermia to the point of hospitalisation), and death or serious injury to those closest to me forcing me to leave the event. I told Julius who the people on this list were; there weren't many, and the top one was Pickle. Anything else and anyone else would have to wait. Anything else and I would just crack on. And I meant that. Completing every single mile of the event on foot meant everything to me.

The first day of that run, 1 June 2022, standing at Land's End, was exactly what I thought it would be like: terrifying, exciting, surreal. In the photos, I look like I am about to start big school. On day one, we ran past the point at which I had DNF-ed the Arc a few months earlier. Hello darkness my old friend …

The thirty-five days that made up this incredible event were some of the happiest, simplest and most joyful of my life. They were also some of the hardest, most painful and difficult. This challenge became the biggest and most important learning curve in this whole period of recovery. Life was completely stripped back. They should prescribe this shit on the NHS. All I had to do was run thirty-five to forty miles a day to get from Land's End to John o'Groats. That is literally all I had to do.

In the first week, I threw everything I knew about mindset out the window. I know. This doesn't sound promising, does it? I decided I was going to try to keep the coaching up and use the rest day for client calls. We got one rest day a week, and a rest day should be just that, rest, but I tried to fill it with 'stuff'. Not only that, but I spent the days I was running thinking about the next day and the next and the next and how I would feel in three weeks. I wasn't being present in the moment and felt pressured and rushed and stressed a lot. At the end of week one, 248 miles in, after an exhausting first rest day in Bristol juggling calls and seeing mates, I finally thought, *Hang on. I'm doing this wrong.* I wasn't doing *any* of the stuff I'd been so focused on learning in recovery. Instead, I was trying to do everything, be everyone and please all the people.

I told my clients I would reschedule calls for when I was back, and I didn't arrange any more socials. I needed to focus solely on me. Part of me worried that would mean I lost money or contracts, or people would think I didn't like them, but I consciously decided to not believe that and try to think something more helpful. What if instead of thinking I was a work-shy freeloader, people thought I was a great example of someone fully focused on what they were doing? What if what I was doing was inspiring my clients? Even though thinking that stuff made me properly cringe, those thoughts were just as likely to have been true as the more unhelpful ones. I used to think multi-tasking was a superpower. Now I *knew* that it was actually just doing two or three things badly and feeling stressed out about it. I put that idea into practice. I began to become the master of owning my attention. And I stopped caring about what other people thought. I reminded myself every single day that I could not control other people's opinions of me, so it was futile even thinking about it, let alone worrying.

The running was fucking hard. While I'd done a lot of multi-day running, I'd never done back-to-back days with this sort of mileage or ascent. Constantly wondering how I would feel the next day, or if I could make it, was exhausting me. And I did know better. When I felt like I was thinking too far ahead about the days, weeks, months, I stopped and looked at where I was and tried to find things to listen to, look at and smell. Instead of worrying, I consciously took in the majesty of the UK's trails during what was an incredibly beautiful sunny June. I concentrated on being fully in the moment. Even though the other runners and I were together in a small group, I wanted to do this alone – and I did. We all did. There were days we ran in silence and days we chatted. We all became a unit – a moving support unit. This was my opportunity to spend over a month putting what I had learnt into practice. And it worked.

The runners – me, my great friend and usual crew member Lorna, Joe, Ross, Rachel, Amanda and Martyn – became a tight-knit family. There was also a support team consisting of James (who ran with us most days) and an ever-revolving door of medics and volunteers. The events company sent staff out every week to crew; I thought it would be awkward, but it wasn't because I reminded myself every day that it wasn't the situation I was in that determined how I felt, it was the thoughts, meanings and interpretations I brought to that situation that mattered. *They're here to help make this a success, not judge you or be your best friend, Allie. Focus on what you can control. Run.*

As the weeks went by, I started to feel different. I felt like a massive weight had been lifted off my shoulders. Although the event was super tough, I felt like I could do it. I was approaching it totally differently to how I'd approached this stuff before. I went through periods over the five weeks where I struggled – of course I did. I hated the road sections, and I was in pain; everyone had some form of anterior tendonitis, and my shins felt like they were physically splitting out of my skin during week three. But I noticed what was happening and brought my attention back to the job in hand – just finish that one day, then get some sleep and reappraise in the morning. Accept how it is, not how you want it to be.

Most days when we finished, I couldn't imagine what the next day would feel like. So I didn't. I just focused on eating, getting clean and going to bed. When the morning came, I just got on with it. When it got to the point where I would cry in the toilet at 6 a.m. – both from pain and fatigue – I told myself to just do one mile and then see how it felt. It always worked. Once immersed, I could just get into the flow of things, and despite it being painful, it would be OK. I had a little mantra I used when my mind started to wander towards the next day: *Don't count the days, make the days count*. And I did, finding a little bit of joy in every single one of them.

Some of the team did get injured to the point that they had started to miss days and sections of the route. Their responses to this were incredible. If I had been in their shoes (or, more relevant, their ice boots), I don't think I would have coped as well. I don't think I was ready for that. Watching how they dealt with injury was so fucking inspiring. They didn't bitch or moan. They didn't feel sorry for themselves. They didn't sulk. They pitched in with the crew, they helped us the best they could, and they showed love, kindness and empathy even though their experience wasn't what they had hoped it would be. I wondered how they did it. I wanted to be that person. I made a point not to forget this and to carry it with me should I end up in the same boat. It was a lesson in humility and performance mindset, and I will never, ever forget it.

On 5 July 2022, myself and the rest of my little team arrived at the white signpost signalling the end of our incredible journey across the UK. One thousand and fifty-three miles run and 89,000 feet of ascent covered. That's three times the height of Everest. We'd all completed our own journey, be it on foot, on foot and in the van, or, for some of us, on foot and on crutches. I'd wondered about how this would feel – we all had – and we'd discussed it at length. But it didn't feel the way any of us thought. On the final day, as I ran along the tiny Scottish roads towards Duncansby Stacks alone, I cried and cried. I kept having to stop to sort my shit out. I was so proud, so fucking relieved. But I was also absolutely devastated that this part of my life was almost over. All the books were right. It's not about the goal. It's about the process. It's about the journey. I didn't want either to end.

The whole team congregated in the tiny car park at Duncansby Head lighthouse – a mere 1.5 miles from our destination – to run the last leg together. We waited at the most north-easterly tip of the UK having run from the most south-westerly. We waited for tears. There were none. We waited for something magic to happen; nothing did. The tourists came and went in their coaches, unaware of what we had achieved. We ate doughnuts and looked sheepishly at the floor. When the whole team was together, we started walking towards the final destination, making lame jokes, sometimes breaking into a jog then realising that would make the end come faster, so slowing down. And then there it was – the iconic signpost surrounded by people taking photos, chatting, going about their normal lives. And us, arriving from what had been an anything-but-normal five weeks, having achieved something that to most people will only ever be a dream. It was over. We had made it.

There were congratulations, a photo or two and some non-alcoholic wine. Nobody on that trip had touched a drop of alcohol for the whole five weeks. I wondered if this was because they knew about my boozehound past. I never asked.

I almost immediately walked away from the group and lay on one of the weird bits of art that you're not supposed to lie on. I waited for some kind of epic feeling to envelop me. Nothing happened. I went to the shop and bought a shiny stone with John o'Groats written on it. Nothing happened. We went for a coffee and got in the van, now filled with balloons, and drove to Duncansby Head to watch the puffins. Nothing happened. Everyone was really quiet. And then we went for dinner and were in bed by 9.30. Still nothing.

The next morning, we left Thurso for Inverness train station. On the drive the radio was on. 'As It Was' by Harry Styles was playing. I could feel myself getting upset. It won't ever be the same as it was. I was scared of going home. I was scared because of what my brain was telling me would happen when I got home. The last time I had got home from a big trip was two days before I decided I wanted to die. I had got home, felt incredibly alone, incredibly scared of being with my own thoughts, drunk a bottle and a half of wine and planned to kill myself. My brain was telling me that was going to happen again. It terrified me. But this time it was different. It was different because I knew what my brain was doing. And I was aware that my past has no effect on my future. I knew that thoughts were just that. Thoughts. *Thoughts alone cannot kill you,* I told myself. It's the feelings and actions that get the results. On that drive home I consciously shifted the thought from, *It's going to happen again,* to, *You're going home to see Pickle. You're going home to see Pickle. You're going home to see Pickle.* I didn't try to reverse the thought, I didn't try to change it. I acknowledged it and put another more helpful thought alongside it. That thought, about Pickle, was the one I chose to focus on and believe. Because I had a choice. We all have choice. And I chose Pickle every time.

Back at home, Julius had covered my house with bunting, and Pickle was, of course, there. Full-body wag, so happy to see me. I obviously started crying again. I had missed her so much. Julius had brought her to me during the first week. She ran with me for a few miles and slept in bed with me and Lorna, cuddling us like a third human, before she'd had to go home. Lorna said it was the best night's sleep she had on the whole trip. That's the power of the Pie cuddle; ask anyone who has been lucky enough to experience it.

Once my front door was shut, and Julius had gone home, I was alone again for the first time in five weeks. Of course, I had my piece of Pie dog, and she was just incredible. But I'd spent thirty-five days living with ten other people. It was a come-down. Pickle is so fucking great, but her conversational skills are sometimes lacking. And the tears came, and the voices started. They told me I was alone because nobody wanted me. They told me I was stupid for expecting something to change just because I'd done this big run. They told me it wasn't a big deal, people did it all the time. They told me that if I couldn't be happy now, after doing something I'd always wanted to do, then I would never be happy. And I sat with them. And I listened to them. And I wrote them all down. And they stayed there in my house with me for about three days. And Pickle sat with them too. And I let them have their say. I let them pass like weather, or cars on a motorway. And I chose, I absolutely *chose,* to *not* believe them. I *chose* to tell myself that the information I was receiving was outdated. There would be some new information soon. I just needed to wait for the new information to be delivered.

The rest of the group were incredible; we checked in on each other via text every day and talked about how hard it was to adjust to real life again. I'd done a fucking good job here – both doing the event and dealing with myself in the aftermath. As the days rolled on, as I wrote my blogs and my thoughts and got back to work, I realised that I was doing OK. I even started to feel grateful, so in all honesty, I didn't finish doing the brain work that I needed to do. When we feel better, we tend to think we don't need to 'do the work' any more, or take the drugs, or see the therapist. But we do. We fucking do. It's a life's work. And there are no hacks. But I'd looked at the calendar. It was just six weeks until the Dragon's Back Race. I told myself I needed to crack on, and instead of really digging into why this event had left me feeling nothing and why reality versus expectation felt so different, I refocused on something else, *another* future goal. Instead of resting my body and my brain, growing a bit, reflecting on what had gone on and doing what I should have been doing, I got straight back at it running. Within five days of being back from my once-in-a-lifetime UK crossing, I was out training again.

Sound the fucking klaxons and get the red bunting out! Isn't this *exactly* how I used to treat running? Isn't this behaviour an example of why I needed to be doing the work I was doing? Did I realise that at the time? Nooooooope. And why was that? Because I was the queen of motivated reasoning.

Motivated reasoning is something that all of us do all the time. It happens when we use reasoning not to come to a conclusion that's true, but to justify the outcome we prefer. The opposite of motivated reasoning is critical thinking. And that was something I had yet to master.

I didn't register that I had a choice as to whether or not to do DBR. I did have a choice. I could have deferred, but old habits die hard, and I reasoned with myself that running the length of the UK was the best training I could do for this race. I reasoned I was the fittest I had ever been, which may have been right. But I was also the most tired I had ever been – and that didn't even come into my brain. I reasoned that it was great training because I *wanted* to do DBR. I also thought that if I'd completed LEJOG, I would be able to complete DBR. Anyone that has done DBR knows that the two are totally incomparable. They are totally different events. The thought that if you can do one you can do the other is literally ridiculous. I hope this is showing you how easy it is to fall into old habits. While I might have been sober, my brain wiring was all over the shop. But this journey is not linear; it's up and down and round and round. I didn't realise that at the time. I thought I was doing everything right. I think I thought I was sorted.

I'd read a lot about the Dragon's Back Race, watched all the films and talked to people who have won it, finished it and DNF-ed it. I'd gone out and done a few recces of the sections I knew presented a problem (aka all of it), and I'd been practising navigation, eating, and packing and repacking and packing and repacking that stupid fifteen-kilo red bag about sixty times. But I was tired. I knew I was tired. I was napping in the day, and runs were hard. The week before the race I did the Grand Tour of Skiddaw – a forty-six-mile race with over 7,000 feet of vert that runs up and down Skiddaw in the Lake District. A few people commented on what a stupid idea this was, but I told them it was a warm-up. A warm-up for what? My impending implosion in the middle of North Wales? I was sliding back into 2017 territory at quite a rate of knots. I am literally bashing my head against the keyboard as I write this. What a knob.

Let's cut to the chase. Dragon's Back chewed me up and spat me out almost immediately. It's brutal. That word, 'brutal', is bandied about a lot, and I really try not to use it, but I think in this instance it's the right word. In an extraordinary administrative fuck-up, someone in the media team had decided that I was one of the seeds for a top three place. I absolutely was not and didn't know where they had got this information from. Before I had even started day one, I was sat in a room with a camera in my face talking like I was going to win the fucking thing. I felt an enormous amount of not only pressure but imposter syndrome from the minute I set foot in camp. I hated it. I wish I'd said no to all of it.

The mornings are early; 6 a.m. is the start time and you're sleeping in a tent with up to seven other people at night – seven people you don't know. There are very strict cut-offs on the route throughout the day. These are for the safety of runners and are non-negotiable. Every single day is unforgiving, but the first two days are renowned for their complexity, danger and terrain. I had renamed northern Snowdonia 'the spiky kingdom' during training, because that's what it is. The rolling hills coming out of Conwy Castle give way to the more punishing ascents, descents and boulder fields of the Carneddau. Once at the top, the descent into the Ogwen Valley is atrocious: huge rocks, boulders and waterfalls making it an almost impossible run for anyone other than the elite mountain runners at the front of the field and the native goats. The ascents and descents of Tryfan and the Glyderau hammer the living shit out of your quads, glutes and lungs and terrify you with their vertiginous edges. The fact the aid stations serve you only water is a killer; you only have the food you have taken with you. No sign of the red ambulance (aka Coca-Cola) unless you've brought it yourself as part of your fifteen-kilo weight allowance. The rules are strict: no crew, no pacers, no marked route, no help. I remember standing on Tryfan during a recce and thinking, *Four miles to Pen-y-Pass – how long can that take?* It took almost three hours. It's like running through the set of *Game of Thrones* up there: extremely hard to navigate and unforgiving underfoot with wet, scree slope inclines you need to use hands and feet to get up, and sharp, spiky slate rocks littering the flatter ridgelines that take you towards the Snowdon horseshoe.

On day one, I went through the Pen-y-Pass checkpoint (the last of the day) with almost an hour and a half to spare. I already felt like shit and had some of the hardest bits of the route still in front of me – the mighty ridge and grade-1 scramble up and over the most feared mountain on the course, Crib Goch, and then a full traverse of the Snowdon horseshoe and the Worst Descent in Wales™ – as I'd named it on my recce day – into camp one. We had a total of fifteen hours to complete day one – which came in at over thirty miles and 13,000 feet of vert. I was cutting it fine.

I got up and over Crib Goch and across Snowdon just as the thunderstorm hit. People had been stopped at Pen-y-Pass and told that their race was over. The weather was turning, and it was getting dark. I'd found a group to go over the horseshoe with, and we stuck together as the clag came in making navigation dangerous and super difficult. Lightning was hitting the hills around us, and I was pretty fucking scared. Then the rain came. I went from pleasantly warm to freezing cold and used every layer I had in my bag. It was starting to get dark. And then my watch ran out of battery.

Thank Christ for my new-found mountain pals. I stuck with them, and they guided me – mainly on my arse – down the pitch-black, slippery, rocky horror of the descent into camp one. I came in with about thirty minutes to spare. And I was fucked.

Once in camp I needed to sort myself out; I was wet, dirty, cold, hungry and exhausted. I felt like I was in a daze. It was hammering it down with rain, and there was nowhere to go to get changed except the tent where people were already sleeping. I didn't want to wake them up. I am so, so used to crew helping on races; on this one they don't. The volunteers that make up the DBR crew are super nice, but they can't, won't and don't give you any special treatment. It felt like everyone else in the race was washed, fed and asleep – mainly because they were – and I was the last person left. Mainly because I was. I could feel proper anxiety rising as I thought about the next day. How the fuck was I supposed to sort my shit out in the dark and the wet in silence *and* feed myself and get enough sleep? I started to panic. I was doing literally the opposite to what I did on my fun-times UK jog: worrying about what was in front of me instead of being in the moment I was in and getting stuff done. On top of that, the people I was running with – my friend Ali M and her friend other Ally (yes, there were three of us) – had been timed out at Pen-y-Pass. *That's what is going to happen to me,* I thought. And thoughts become results.

I managed to get to sleep at around 1 a.m. and woke up four hours later. I was fucking exhausted. Way more exhausted than I had been on my last long multi-day. Maybe because then I was getting eight hours of sleep a night and wasn't in a fucking tent? And maybe because I didn't start that event off the back of another 1,000-mile event. At the time I couldn't see this; I just started to have a massive go at myself for being shit. I saw everyone else in that event as better than me – more qualified to be there. I faffed that morning and left at 6.20 instead of 6 a.m. And that was part of my downfall.

I couldn't stop thinking about the sections I'd not recced. They were coming up that morning and the following day. Two small sections I had not seen: Cnicht and Cader Idris. It was all I could think of. *That's going to fuck me,* I thought. I wasn't in the mile I was in, I was in miles I had no idea about. I wasn't playing to win, I was playing not to lose.

The day started out OK, and I was running at a decent pace, but as we approached Cnicht I started to realise that things were going to get a lot more difficult. There were three ascents, not just one. The elites set out later than us norms and were flashing past, running effortlessly up and down the hills. It was fucking windy, I was dying on my arse and I felt like an idiot. I knew what was coming; I had done the second part of today and knew that there were some extremely challenging boggy sections followed by some horrendous climbs and very sketchy navigation across the extremely remote and confusing Rhinogydd mountain range. I pressed on, and at the first checkpoint of the day asked the crew if they thought I would make it before the 3 p.m. cut-off. Yes, they said, no problem. I didn't believe them. I knew that the bogs would kill me. And they did.

I was about a mile from the second checkpoint when the clock struck 3 p.m. I knew it was the end of my race. I walked that mile in tears. Tears of frustration, tears of anger, tears of relief maybe? I was met by Stu Smith – one of the safety team and a man I absolutely love. I'd worked with Stu on a number of events before; he was the man responsible for getting me over my fear of mountains and ridges, and he always had a kind word, a good hug and a brew on the go. He is also one of the most intelligent and skilled mountain safety leaders I know. I would trust Stu with my life, and I'm so glad that he was there. I burst into tears, got a hug and went and sat by the river with him, smoking cigarettes (me not him) and just feeling like an abject failure. Feeling like everyone was laughing at me. Feeling like this was the end of the world. I'd fucked it on day two.

There's an option with DBR to keep going as non-competitive if you time out. Nowadays this is called the 'hatchling course'; back then it was called 'hanging about because nobody will pick you up and you're a fucking loser'. I was stuck in North Wales with no real way of getting out, and so that's what I did. I assumed that I would have to do half-days – assumed not asked – and that was a mistake. The following day I got in the bus of sadness with the other losers (this is absolutely a reflection of how I felt at the time and not what the bus was actually called or who was in it) and was driven to Machynlleth – the halfway point for day three – and told to wait for the elites to come through before we could start running. We could go to the local cafes and get food – and a lot of the other competitors did. I just sloped about like a sad, spoilt brat, phoned my mum and cried a lot. I'd obviously taken nothing from the stoicism that I'd seen from my injured comrades on my previous adventure. It was agony waiting to be able to start, walking around the village with that number on, knowing that I had failed. It was agony when people came and asked, 'Oh, are you doing Dragon's Back?', and I had to say no, I'd fucked it and was now non-competitive. I was using none of the skills that I'd been learning at home from the books, the therapy or the coaching. I was just allowing the old stories to run riot and believing them. I was behaving like a giant baby.

I did the half-day Wednesday and the full day Thursday, but on Friday, sitting in a vehicle waiting to be released on to the Bannau Brycheiniog for the second half of day five, some very Welsh rain lashing down against the windows and with one of the other Alis making it very clear she wanted to go home, I caved and pulled the plug. The Queen had died, and we weren't even going to run into Cardiff Castle – and I was just a thirty-minute drive from my sister's house. I'd had enough, seen enough, done enough. I was exhausted from the mental flogging I was giving myself and, well, just from everything. I made the call and went home.

Do I wish I'd done it differently and stayed? Not really, no. I'd fallen so far down the knowing–doing gap that I didn't know how to get out. I didn't actually enjoy DBR, and that was on me. When you're at the back from the off and fighting for survival, there's not a lot of camaraderie to be had because there's no time for it. Everyone is fighting their own battle; it's an incredibly individual challenge, not what I was used to, and I wasn't prepared for it at all. You have to absolutely focus on yourself to get through it, and I hadn't done that either. I spent a lot of time comparing myself to other people, worrying about the next day instead of being in the one I was in and worrying about the other Ali – just like I worry about my crew.

Now I knew what it would take to complete that race because I'd done a good fifty per cent of it, and the later stages I didn't complete I knew well from running them socially with my sister and during other races. I also knew something else. I was not physically strong enough. My legs just didn't have the strength to get up and over those mountains at any sort of pace. Yes, I was tired, but even on fresh legs it would have been a big ask. I had spent my entire running life avoiding strength and conditioning, and that was very apparent here. My quads and glutes were just destroyed by the Welsh terrain. My arse was *literally* handed to me. It was never going to happen.

I was absolutely devastated to have not finished DBR – but I wasn't even close. Out on day two – no fucking chance. Despite not using my mental toolbox and despite not doing what I knew, I accepted that this was totally on me. I needed to be stronger physically and more robust mentally. I needed to do more work on my thought process and take notes on where it had gone wrong over that week. So I decided to make that my number two priority (sobriety is *always* number one) after I'd finished licking my wounds – which took me about two weeks.

So, here was a person with a 100 per cent completion rate on all races as a depressed alcoholic, DNF-ing two races in a year as a sober slightly-less-depressed-aholic – albeit two fucking hard ones. Now as I sit here and write this, I believe that those DNFs were incredibly important to my recovery; they had to happen. Maybe on some level I made them happen. Long term, they were both lessons in acceptance and kindness towards myself that I couldn't learn without having gone through the painful, shitty bit. And these DNFs absolutely weren't the end of anything. They were the start.

They were lessons in understanding that just because I'd read something, just because I coached people on it, that didn't mean that it was part of the fabric of me, or that I understood how to use it. You have to live that stuff, you have to really make the effort to process it and put it into practice every single day for it to make a difference, and *that* takes time. You have to build an incredibly strong bridge across the knowing–doing gap by repeatedly doing the work while being conscious of doing the work. That's where the proper graft is with this stuff. And running, cycling, mountain climbing, whatever you choose to do, is the perfect place to test it all.

This was work that I was absolutely going to dedicate myself to. I was going to dedicate myself to doing it, teaching it and living it.

CHAPTER 9
DEAR READER (PROTECT YOUR MAGIC)

Listen to: 'Yes' – McAlmont & Butler

Hi. Hello. Dear Reader,

I sit here just over two years sober. And I've just given up smoking. I know. I'm just a few plant-based choices away from being fucking perfect and highly irritating. It is July 2023 and I'm in a little flat in Skinningrove on the north-east coast of Yorkshire with Pickle. We've come here to finish the book off. I can't do it at home. I get too distracted. Here, I can spend the early mornings on the beach with her and the evenings doing the same, and attempt to finish this fucker off by slotting writing blocks in between those important Pie times. Sometimes I need a bit of space from the words. The beach helps with that. It's been a really rocky road getting all this on paper, and I've learnt I need to be kind and patient with myself in the process. It's all about protecting your magic.

I've ummed and ahhed about the best way to finish this off. I want it to be as helpful as it can be, but at the same time, I know you're not a fucking idiot. If you wanted a self-help book, you would have bought one. So I thought I'd write you a letter. It's the best way to get across how I've managed to get to where I am now – which is a pretty contented place, albeit with the metaphorical potholes on the drive and cupboards still full of things I need to consider getting rid of. I am not fixed, I am not perfect, and I still get very, very sad, angry and occasionally just fucking upset about stuff, but honestly, I am in a better place than I could have ever hoped to have been a couple of years ago. And that's amazing, isn't it? I thought I'd write to you with a bit of background on how that's happened. There might be some bits that you find useful here. I really hope so. I wish someone had written me a letter.

First though, a little catch-up on where I'm at because it's been a while and I've done some stuff. After that DBR DNF I sulked for about two weeks and then had a proper look at my running and realised I was in danger of returning to 2017 territory – repeating the same mistakes and expecting different outcomes. I was running too much, stacking events together, not actually doing the basics that well and still defining my worth through whether or not I finished events. This was a comfortable place for me; I was used to it. It was an easy cycle to fall back into. But I recognised it, and I knew it had to change, so that was a win. I reframed that experience from embarrassing horror show to the start of Project Fuck Chi, Draig. That's 'fuck you, dragon' in Welsh. I'm still trying to learn Welsh. *Ei galed gwaedlyd.*

I fucked up that race for a million reasons. I was nowhere near strong or fast or confident enough across that terrain, so I am doing something about it. I joined a gym, and I am getting strong. I've been doing it for just over a year, and it's made a massive difference. I am super proud of myself. For years I'd told myself that I hated gyms because they were full of bellends. But as well as bellends, at gyms, it turns out, there are also people like me, who just want to improve their fitness or maybe train for something specific. I've got really good at looking at my thoughts with curiosity and asking if certain thoughts I have are limiting me. The thought about gyms and bellends was. So I became a gym bellend. I don't like how I look now, it's not the way I want to look, but instead of telling myself I'm bigger than I was before, I tell myself I'm getting fitter and stronger. Because that's how I want to think about my body; it's an incredible machine and it deserves respect. So does yours, reader. Write that down and put it somewhere you can see it.

I plan to return to Wales for my second go at slaying the Dragon when I am absolutely ready to do that. I'll do the work and I'll finish that course. I'll make sure I enjoy the process, and as much as I want to finish, it won't matter if I get to the end or not. I want to feel strong and like I am doing a good job. I'll get there eventually. You only fail when you stop trying, and I've not stopped trying yet.

What else has happened? Oh yeah ... in January of this year I went back to the Arc of Attrition and finished it. It took me thirty-two hours. I was thrilled. I felt so, so proud when I crossed that line; it was a proper moment for me. Pickle was there and I cried. I really appreciate being able to feel feelings again – even the shit ones. It's something I will always feel grateful for. You don't know how good it is to feel everything until you've felt nothing, and that's not a situation I would advise getting into. If you are in that situation now, know that it does get better. But you have to make the changes to get there. And you can. You can choose to do that with your mind.

After the Arc, in April I took part in and won (WON!) my first 200-mile race. The Wild Horse 200 is a non-stop epic that crosses the mighty Bannau Brycheiniog in South Wales, from Chepstow to Worm's Head. It was a turning point in my life. Another one. They are happening all the time at the moment, these little turning points, these little moments of magic; sometimes they're hard to keep up with, sometimes they're painful, sometimes they're joyous, but the most important thing is they're there and it's important to recognise them as wins – no matter how small. I'd advise you to do the same; have a look at your life and just take notice of the tiny wins – even a parking space at the supermarket counts. Tiny wins make you happier and add up to big changes in your brain chemistry. Am I annoying you yet? I'm fucking annoying myself.

I think the result of the Wild Horse was down to two things: the gym work to get me physically strong, and the brain work I've done to get me as well as I can be. I've included a bit about that race as an epilogue at the end of this book. I hope it doesn't seem boring or braggy. A lot of the books I've read use metaphors for illustrating change, but the Wild Horse wasn't a metaphor, it was something that actually happened. It was a situation that showed me how far I have come and allowed a little glimpse towards where I could go. I turned that race around not once, but twice. And I did that with my brain – the same brain that for years told me I was a piece of shit and tried to kill me. Don't you think that's a magical thing to be able to do? Well, here's the thing: you can do it too. We all can.

The rest of the year has been a bit like reading a shipping forecast. Variable, occasionally rough. Good, occasionally moderate. Showers. Rain later. That's the human condition. It's learning how to ride the waves in our wonky boats that is the key to staying afloat. And I am learning to do that every day. I wanted to write to you, person to person, to explain a bit about how I am doing that and impart some of the things I have learnt that have really helped me. I'm hoping they will help you get your shit together if you need to, help you keep it together if you don't, or possibly help you to help someone else. I wonder how you really are. Please don't just say OK if you're not.

Whatever state you're in, know that you are loved, even if you don't feel like you are. Stephen Fry once wrote, 'Although they mean well, it's sometimes quite galling to be reminded how much people love you when you don't love yourself that much' (*Letters of Note*). Stephen was right. He's always right. Love bounces off you when you don't appreciate yourself. A lot of love bounced off me before I accepted help. I was Teflon-coated for years. I am scared that I still don't really believe in romantic love. I don't trust it and it scares me. But at least I am aware of that. Could do without crying in Aldi about it, though.

I have found Post-its to be my new best friends. I have fucking hundreds of them, all over my house. I started writing lines from books that helped me, things that people had told me or messages I needed to believe on them, and putting them where I could see them, and it's become a bit of an obsession. Whether it's those instructions on washing my face and cleaning my teeth before I go to bed on the bathroom mirror (yes, I still need to remind myself), or more urgent beliefs I need to change, there are little luminous squares stuck everywhere. Sticking them somewhere I can see them helps get any message I need to hear across. And yes, sometimes I do feel like ripping those Post-its down and throwing them in the bin. If I do that, I just write a new one later. It's OK to rip things up and throw them in the bin. I did it with all my Take That posters when Robbie left. It was a ballache getting them out the bin a few days later. I think that was my earliest lesson in reaction versus response ...

Acceptance of everything has been key to me getting better – both in life and running. I read Brad Stulberg's book *The Practice of Groundedness*, and it really did change my life a bit. He's big on acceptance, is Brad, and now, so am I. Accepting where you are actually at in life and what is actually going on is really fucking hard, but without it you can't go anywhere. If life isn't great, sometimes you have to be really vulnerable and brave to accept why that might be. Sometimes it can take a rock bottom to do that, but it doesn't have to be that way. I'd advise you to read that book. It's a banger. If Brad started a cult, I'd join.

Vulnerability, asking for help, whatever you want to call it, is not a weakness, it's a strength. To be able to open it all up to someone – and I mean *all* of it – is the bravest and most freeing thing you can do. Find the right person, whether that's a trained therapist or your best mate or even your dog. You will know when you find the right person because they will offer to help you by actually asking if you are OK. Think about how many times people ask you if you're OK during the day. Think about how many times you lie to people about being OK. It's kind of fucked up. Be absolutely honest with them. Ask them to listen and not try to help. Free yourself. Be honest. Be Brave.

If you feel like a burden, if your thoughts feel like burdens, start by saying them out loud when you are alone, or writing them down. Once they are said out loud, written down or shared, thoughts lose all their weight. They become neutral. They are just words. That's why people scream in the woods. That's why I talk to Pickle. Remember that you are the thinker, not the thought. That's powerful. Buy yourself a notebook. Use it.

People think journalling is writing down bad thoughts and replacing them with good ones. That's not what it is. Journalling can be whatever you want it to be. In my early recovery, mine had the day, how many days I'd been sober and what I had done that day. It didn't have how I felt, because I felt nothing. As I started to feel better, I did start writing how I felt – and then came the anger. There's some proper scary stuff in there, but I had to get it out and I'm so glad I did. Nowadays my journalling is a lot more psychological, but yours can be whatever you want it to be. Mine is me trying to work out the arguments I have with myself in a very grown-up manner. But it might go back to the angry rants at some point. There's no right or wrong way to do it. If you feel like you have nothing to write, then write, 'I have nothing to write.' You'll soon be writing again.

I found that seeing my words on a page made it easier to say them to someone. Start the conversation by asking the person you have trusted to listen, to listen without judgement and not to try to solve the problem. Tell them what you want. Do you want them to help, or do you want them to listen? Listening is an underrated skill; we have two ears and one mouth. We should use them to that ratio, and not many people do. If you can't find anyone in your circle to talk to, or if you feel like you don't have a circle, I've made a list of places on page 172 where you can find someone to listen to you. Be brave. Take that first step. Read your journal down the phone to a stranger if you have to. Or even start with your dog. There is hope. I promise you.

If you're the reader who has searched these pages looking for help for someone you love, tell them that you want to listen to them, and do just that. You may have to tell them this hundreds of times before they take you up on it. Most of the time people don't want to be fixed, they want to be heard. People had to tell me hundreds of times they wanted to help, but it didn't matter because I didn't want to help myself; that might be why you need to keep asking. There's a difference between desire and decision, and that difference is often fear. I was scared that people would make me stop doing things I thought I loved – like drinking. Or tell me I was mad and section me. Ultimately, they did neither. It was my choice to stop drinking and change my behaviour. Mine and mine alone, and it came from feeling safe. Ask the people you love what they are scared of. Ask yourself what you are scared of. It's a conversation starter. It could start a conversation that will save someone's life.

When people do talk to you, you might not agree with what you're being told, but don't argue against it. Just listen without prejudice. Listen without judgement. I am still learning that words are neutral; it's our thoughts and feelings about them that give them meaning. Mind-blowing but true. Zoom out and observe words. There's a time and place for your opinion, and listening to someone when they're being vulnerable isn't it. You have the power to make someone feel heard and safe. Remember that. It's powerful. It's magical. It's a gift.

One of the driving forces for me getting help, one of the things that really helped me understand what was going on, was reading about other people's experiences, and that is why I wrote this book. I always picked up books about fucked-up people or situations to make my life feel a bit more normal or manageable. My favourite books are *A Little Life* (fiction), *A Million Little Pieces* (did we ever get to the bottom of whether this is fiction or not?) and *Man's Search for Meaning* (definitely not fiction). What a collection. These books made me feel like it was OK to be sad, that my pain was shared. They made me feel seen. They made me feel heard. When I started to realise that I had a big drinking problem, and as I came out of addiction, my appetite for shared experience through reading became voracious. I read so much. Sometimes all it takes is that feeling of identifying with someone else's story to be the precursor for change. I've included highlights from my reading list at the end of my book – my book which I hope helps you or someone you know in the same way as the ones I've listed helped me.

When it comes to change, it's not about needing to change, it's about wanting to – so asking yourself and others questions like, 'What do you want to do?' is more helpful than suggesting someone get help. You or they may want to do nothing, and that is OK as well. People respond better to change when it is their idea. I did when it was mine.

People are allowed to feel like shit, even if it appears they have it all. You are allowed to feel like shit, even if you feel like you have it all. Life is fifty per cent shit. That's a fact. We need to have the shit bits to enjoy the good bits. It's OK to feel bored, it's OK to feel like you're coasting. Contrary to popular social-media-led belief, life is not great all the time and it never will be. Remember what I wrote about acceptance? Accept it. If you expect a unicorn existence, you will be very disappointed. Wallow in boredom; it's a first-world privilege. Know what toxic positivity is and avoid it at all costs. Sadness, boredom and even apathy are not bad things. They are neutral things, and they are inevitable parts of our existence. Enjoy feeling them. Be grateful you can. This is your life.

Know that you cannot control what other people think about you and it's none of your fucking business anyway. Seeking external validation, especially in regard to your self-worth, is a futile and damaging habit, but one pretty much all of us revel in. I am trying to take note of when I do it, and I still do it a lot. Interestingly, since I have started noticing myself doing it more and more, my social media usage has taken a hammering. I don't feel like I need those likes and comments any more and try to only use it if I have something really helpful to say. Try it, reader; see what happens when you stop giving a fuck about what people online think. Then transfer it to real life.

We love being told we're doing well, we love a medal, we love people commenting on how fast or far we have run, or how fit we are, and we love praise and attention – of course we do. But no matter how many people tell you you're brilliant, no matter how many races you win, no matter how many miles you run, likes you get or people you fuck, the only opinion that truly matters is yours. If you think you're a piece of shit, if you think you're worth nothing, then that is how you will feel. External validation means nothing if you don't like yourself to start with. To paraphrase Brad Stulberg, stop trying to be the best at everything and aim to be the best at getting better at a few things. Being able to validate yourself, to say well done to little old you at the end of the day, and to revel in your little wins, is an invaluable skill and it is completely possible. I congratulate myself every time I finish that two-litre bottle of water on my desk. Job well done. When I make the bed – thanks, Allie, you'll really enjoy that bed later! On to the next little win. I appreciate I'm doing the basics well. I have even started to congratulate myself when I fuck up – for noticing I've fucked up and responding instead of reacting. Learn how to do this and life becomes full of tiny wins. And tiny wins become great big, massive ones.

Back to neutrality. See circumstances as just circumstances. Because that is what they are. Circumstances do not define our outcomes. It's how we think, feel and respond to circumstances that matters. I see you shaking your head at this, reader, I see you. Do some experiments; see what happens, be open-minded and curious. You'll soon see what I mean. A pissing-wet, windy day does not mean a bad day. It means a great opportunity to do some bad-weather training. It means getting those jobs you needed to get done at home done. It means testing out your new jacket. You have a choice when it comes to how you think about everything and anything. And because you have a choice about what you think, you also have a choice about how you feel. Nobody makes you feel anything. Your thoughts about people, places, weather, comments, everything – that's what makes you feel. And you don't have to feel good. Go back and read what I said about feeling shit. That's a choice too!

For a long time I thought that along with being properly depressed, I was just a negative thinker; that I was just sad and damaged and programmed that way – a helpless product of my environment and upbringing. But that isn't entirely true. Yes, my cognitive bias swings in favour of the bleak, but I now know I have the ability to ask how helpful believing that stuff is. Now I can respond to it. For years and years I had no idea that I had a choice in the thoughts I believed and acted on. When we are little, we don't have this self-awareness, but as we get older we do. Unlocking it is a superpower. It's really helped me to start writing new stories for myself – ones that are helpful. How have I learnt this? Therapy, coaching, reading and doing the work. There is no better investment than therapy and coaching. Both things have changed my life and continue to do so.

I am learning to be patient with my mind and my body, and I try to allow absolute rest for both. I have never done this before. I was raised to think doing nothing makes you lazy. It does not. You need rest to grow. Growth doesn't happen while you're running a thirty-mile training run or lifting weights in a gym or reading the complete works of Shakespeare. It happens afterwards, when you actually rest. If I feel guilty or panic about resting, I remind myself that those feelings come from thoughts, and thoughts are not facts. I cherish rest now. I cherish silence. I make time to sit with Pickle and do nothing for two hours in the evenings. I make time to sit in front of the TV. It's as important as the work, the gym stuff and the training runs. Resting does not make you a bad or lazy person, your thoughts about it do. Resting makes you strong.

Stop asking yourself, 'When will it get better/easier/nicer?', and concentrate on right here, right now. At the start of my recovery, I had to do this because I could no longer see a future. Minute by minute, day by day, I dealt with it as it came. This was both with regard to my stopping drinking and the recovery of my mental health. I didn't realise I was learning to be in the moment, but I was. I try to do this every day. I'm not always successful, but I'm aiming for progress, not perfection, and most of the time it works. While I make plans to do things, I no longer 'look forward' to doing them. I know they're coming, I prepare for them with joy, but I really try to live in the minute I am in, giving full attention to what is actually happening right now rather than what I think might happen. I've also started using this idea for my big-girl, super-long races. There is no point wondering how I will feel at the next aid station, it's about how I feel now. If I feel great, then that's great. If I don't feel great, I'll sort it out and crack on. If I can't sort it out, I'll stop. Stop trying to predict the future and just go and create it. Preferably after a sandwich and a salt tablet.

If you allow your worth to be defined by anything other than the fact it is a given, you're skating on thin ice. I attempted to define mine through sex, relationships, friendships, jobs, famous people, other people's opinions and behaviour (both perceived and actual), the quality of my leather jacket, how many Access All Areas passes I had, how many world firsts I had, 100-mile races, the fact I shopped at Waitrose occasionally – you name it, I fucking used it. I used so many external factors as a hook on which to hang my self-worth that I'm not surprised it brought the wall down.

Self-worth is the level of importance that you put on yourself – which in itself sounds wank, but when you really fucking hate yourself, you will naturally look for external validation as to why you should be allowed to roam this wonderful planet. When you don't find it, it's bridge-jumping time. It really does come from inside you. For me, nowadays, it comes from my values. If I am meeting them to the best of my ability, then I'm OK. If I am not, then I calmly work out why and adjust. While it's lovely to know that I am helping people with my job, this book, etc., it really comes down to my opinion of me. Unfortunately, I have that live-in nightmare lodger depression who can make that difficult, but because I see him as a person, a living thing, he really becomes an external factor too, so he's not going to define my worth either. Sure, he can have his opinion and I will listen to it, but he's not defining shit. I do that. Me. From inside. I have a choice, and I choose this way of thinking. I have the word *Worthy* tattooed on my arm to remind me that I am.

You are worthy of love, respect and a place here too, regardless of your 10k time or how many parkruns you've done. That stuff doesn't mean shit. Knowing your worth protects your magic. Your magic is what makes you worthy.

Back at the start of this book I talked about a shiny box that I felt was buried deep inside me. I didn't want to call it a soul or a spirit, because that creeps me out, but through the writing down of all this stuff, I have come to refer to it as my magic (which also sounds creepy, but we'll go with it). We all have a bit of magic in us – that thing that you can't put your finger on that makes us, well, us I suppose. It is always there underneath, regardless of our behaviours, our addictions, our depression or anxieties or traumas. You have it and the people you love have it, and if you don't protect it, you risk losing it. I don't know how it gets there or where it comes from, but when I think back to me as a really little girl, dressing up like a mentalist, making people laugh at parties with quite incredible impressions of Margaret Thatcher and Frank Spencer, telling made-up jokes, being super confident, witty, sarcastic, creative, precocious, I see it. It's still there. Have a think about yours. Write down what your magic looks like, and if you're not sure, ask someone else. It will make you smile, I promise.

Your magic is the thing that people like the most about you. It's the thing they want around them – your vibe, aura, whatever you want to call it. It's what you bring to the party, it's what makes you special and unique. These days I see my magic as my superpower and I've got to the point where I recognise it to be the thing that I guard above all else. My magic is fuelled by my sobriety. My magic was there from the day I was born. I absolutely believe that. I wasn't a drinker when I was born, I became one. I wasn't an addict when I was born, I became one. I wasn't depressed when I was born, I became depressed. All these things dimmed my light a bit. Protect your magic, because it can and will be dulled by your behaviour and by the effects of the behaviour of other people. Sometimes it can even be almost extinguished altogether.

When that happens, the people that don't matter – some of whom may have told you they love you, some of whom may have had a hand in dulling your magic – will disappear. And them doing that will only go on to dim it further. Do not ignore those red flags and tiny voices telling you that maybe what's going on with you isn't right. Create boundaries and stick to them. Be careful who you surround yourself with. Be careful who you share your magic with. Be careful with yourself. Value your magic above all else. Without you and without it there is nothing else. I know you think I am mental. Maybe I am. But I know what I mean. And I think you might as well.

That's a lot, isn't it? Sorry, this letter has gone on for fucking ages.

This is everyday, ongoing work for me. Sometimes my brain fights against the changes I am trying to make. Our brains hate change, and that's OK. Our brains are there to protect us from harm, and I'm grateful mine is working correctly. Even addiction is our brain's way of trying to save us from harm – which is super fucked up, but that's how it works. Sometimes I find myself saying, 'It's OK, nothing is going to hurt you', out loud, to my brain. It helps calm it down. Try it. It works. That, and a couple of deep breaths.

I have accepted that while I may never be perfect, free from depression or the greatest ultrarunner in the world, and while I will always be in recovery from addiction, that is all OK. It's all good stuff. I can use these circumstances to help other people. All these parts that make me who I am don't mean that I am broken, unworthy or binnable. They make me uniquely qualified to write this book, do my workshops, coach my clients and do all the other things I want to do. That's cool, right? We're all uniquely qualified, no matter how fucked up we are.

All this stuff I have waffled on about does change your life. Not in a winning £15 million way. But in a more subtle way. When I started to really do the work, when I started being kind to myself, accepting myself as I was and not trying to be something that I wasn't, not trying to hide behind alcohol or another persona, my life did begin to change. My coaching business, which I started more out of desperation than anything else, started to and continues to flourish. I now spend my days helping people achieve their dreams. I don't have another job. This is it. This is my career, and I made that happen. I literally get paid to do what I love. And there's some other stuff too.

In 2022, I was asked to join the inov-8 team as a sponsored athlete, joining the likes of Damian Hall and Nicky Spinks on the Lake District-based running brand's books. They give me kit; I wear it and tell them if it works or not. Luckily most of the time it does. I am incredibly grateful for their support. They have never, ever asked me to be a better runner, win shit or be someone I am not. In the same year I was named one of the *Guardian*'s top twenty most inspiring female adventurers, and the *Times* published a full-page article on my little jog across the UK. In 2023, I was asked to join the Centurion ultrarunning team – not because I am fast, break records or am an elite athlete, but because I am me. And being me is good enough. I was also shortlisted for a *TGO* award – Outdoor Personality of the Year, if you must know – and was followed around the Arc of Attrition by a film crew making a film about the people that go back for more after a DNF. These things happened not through luck or good fortune; they happened because I made a decision to stop fucking destroying myself through alcohol and sort my shit out. They happened because I made them happen.

And then, dear reader, there's this book. I was told by many people, repeatedly, that I wouldn't get a publisher. That Person even told me it was a pipe dream. But I kept writing, just like I kept doing the work on my brain. And then, in 2022, I met someone on a hill during a race in the Lake District. I got talking to her and she helped me get these words on to paper and into your hands. Not because she liked me, not because she thought I was funny when I was drunk and not because I was lucky, but because I wrote a good book. I stuck with it even when it was really fucking hard. You have to believe that you have nothing to lose and everything to gain from being brave and taking action. You have to believe that. (She does think I'm funny, though … let's get that one straight.)

And so, as our final chat ends, dear reader, I leave you with this final bit of insight. I guess what I am saying is that there is time to sort your shit out. There is time to help that person you love and there is hope.

During the writing of this story, I sometimes felt like I was watching my life play out on a screen, staring, appalled, as I almost drank myself to death then tried to prove I was OK by hammering my fragile body race after race after race. I have felt like I was watching through my fingers as I made mistake after mistake, as I ignored warnings and repeated behaviours, as I was vile to people I loved, as I treated members of my own family, my friends, my partners and even people I didn't know like pieces of shit. I have felt guilt, shame, horror and embarrassment as I have gone through this process, and I have had to get down on my knees and ask for forgiveness on countless occasions.

While running didn't save me, every single mile I have run has taught me something. When I started running, I think a lot of the time I just wanted to find that peace – to run towards momentary peace, away from the person I was. I've said it before – now I see it as running towards the person I want to be.

Until you push yourself to do these sometimes-terrifying things, you will never come face to face with who you really are, what you are capable of, or what you could potentially be. We live in a world hell bent on distracting us from our thoughts. A world that tells us only to think good ones. Without distraction, when you are in an endurance situation, alone, with no phone reception or WiFi or way out, it is then that you see who you really are, even just for a few moments. Those moments, sometimes hundreds of them, pieced together, can be enough to change your life. When you decide it's time to notice those red flags (which you will, in your own time) you will discover something amazing. Running helps do that. Running will buy you time. Running will buy you clarity. Running will buy you self-respect and teach you self-care. Running will always lead you to living a life less ordinary. Running will help you understand that you are enough. But let me be clear for the final time: running alone will not save you. Only you have the power to do that. I firmly believe that my best days of running are ahead of me – my biggest adventures and my best results. I believe that, because I now live a life that I never thought was possible – one of acceptance and freedom rather than constriction and fear.

I don't see a wall any more. There is no wall. I don't see it when I am running, and I don't see it in any other part of my life. People will tell you it's there; they'll say they've seen it, felt it, hit it. Sometimes it might feel like it's there, but it's just not. The Wall is a thought, a belief, and belief, by its very definition in the *Oxford English Dictionary,* is 'the acceptance that something exists or is true, often without proof'. Like I said at the start, the stories we believe are the ones we tell ourselves the most. Maybe it's time to really look at yours.

On the wall in my office is a neon sign that reads, *The World is Yours*. Stop waiting to be ready. You will never be ready. You are ready now. And the world is yours.

Thank you for reading this. What you do with it now is up to you.

A x

EPILOGUE

BLOG EXCERPT: UNTIL YOU'RE BROKEN, YOU DON'T KNOW WHAT YOU'RE MADE OF – TAMING THE WILD HORSE 200

Published 11 April 2023
Age: 42
Months sober: 21
Years running: 15
Listen to: 'The Whole of the Moon' – The Waterboys

It was raining. The ascent out of that checkpoint was nothing short of cunty. My feet were killing me. I needed my dry shoes. I had forty miles until I would see my crew. It was dark. I was on my own, I was hungry, I was going to get overtaken. At the last checkpoint a volunteer had told me I was leading the ladies race and all hell had broken loose in my head.

Hang on, what the fuck was that? Going to get overtaken? WHO FUCKING CARES? And there we go. Round and round. Using energy I didn't have to fight with myself. The dawn broke; it was rubbish and grey. I was seventy-five miles in, and I was hating every single second. Everything hurt. I was being a super-horrible arsehole to myself. My battery felt like it was drained to about five per cent. I had been running for twenty-four hours and only got seventy-five miles into a 200-mile race. What a fucking loser. I felt like I was hobbling about like a drunk person. I felt like I did when I DNF-ed the Arc the first time. I remember telling some people that I caught up with, what a shit time I was having. I really regret infecting them with my bad vibes – sorry, guys. And then I sat down. And then I had a really honest conversation with myself. It went a bit like this.

'Allie. What are you doing? Come on. You have trained so hard for this. You have put so much time, effort and money into this. This is your life. You are living your life RIGHT NOW IN THIS MOMENT *and you are ruining it by not switching on and having a calm conversation with yourself. Nobody expects anything of you, and if they do, that's on them. It's nothing to do with you. I know you feel tired, I know you feel stressed out, but it's all manageable. You are hungry. You know you are. Let's sort this out, shall we? Let's get you some proper food. Text Lorna. Call Julius. Arrange to meet them on the course. Arrange for them to meet you earlier. We can manage this together and get you a sandwich. I know your stomach is upset, but we can sort that out with proper food. Nobody died from shitting themselves on a race. At least I don't think anyone has. We can google that later.* ANYWAY *listen to me, Allie. Listen. You just need to keep going to the next* CP *then make a decision. Things can change. You know they can. I promise you that things can feel better. Remember: you are doing the best you can and that is enough. Can I just mention this first lady thing? That's great, but it's not defining your worth. None of this does. You're doing fucking great. Other people's opinions are their opinions. You're here to enjoy yourself. Remember? You love this place. You love running, you love the challenge. It's OK you're finding it hard – it is hard! So find it hard, wallow about in it and suck it up. You can't pay for this type of experience, can you? You're in it. Feel the feelings! Rejoice that you can feel the feelings! None of it – not winning, not being fast – none of it makes you any more or less worthy as a person. Just do you. You are ace just how you are – even when you're being a brat. OK? Now*

let's get up and get to this next checkpoint. Come on. Give yourself a cuddle, and let's go.'

And that is sitting in discomfort. This is what all the books I read talk about; this is what all the practice I have done on my brain looks like in a real-life case study. This is me unfucking it. This is me turning it around. You can't buy this sort of experience. You have to live it. This is what years of pain and fear of failure and self-hatred look like when they are healing. And when you do it, when you put it into practice, when it starts to work – that is so, so powerful. I gave myself a cuddle, chose to think, I just have to get to that checkpoint, and I got to checkpoint four.

When I got there, I ordered two Pot Noodles and cuddled a dog I found outside. Rachel (second lady) came in and I chatted to her because she is lovely and sorted my feet out and moaned a lot. Neither of us mentioned placings. We never mentioned it. She left before me, and I happily waved her off. Rachel is an incredible runner. She's done astonishing things. In the time I spent with her I thought she was ace. I'll go when I am ready, I thought. That's fucking cool. Total mindset change. It's food, I thought. Lack of food sends me mad.

I thanked the incredible volunteers and got on my way. Leg five was underway – up Tor y Foel we go!

I met Lorna and Kirsten at about 100 miles and had coffee and a bagel – more food! And then ran on. Ran. I was still running 100 miles in. I was so chuffed that I felt so strong. I stopped for five minutes for another lunch and marvelled at the beauty of where I was. I felt grateful to the environment and grateful to myself. What a way to live your life, Allie. You lucky, lucky bastard.

Time passed and the 'I don't want to eat' message started again. I was really struggling with food. But that calm conversation came into play again. Come on, Allie, you have to get food down. Even if it comes up you have to get it down. Do your best. Salt tablet, food, keep calm. If you're sick, you will have at least absorbed a bit of food. Do your best to get some food down. So I did. I kept eating despite everything that touched my lips making me gag. Despite my whole being saying no, I managed to get food down. I wasn't sick again until much later. But now, the hallucinations had started.

Fast forward a number of pretty fucked-up miles, not all of which I can remember …

I was now sixty hours and 140 miles into the race. Up until this point I'd had about ninety minutes' sleep. I didn't want to tell Julius (who was pacing me) what was happening because I didn't want an intervention, but about six miles outside Pen-clawdd it all fell to shit. Everything was moving now. The bins jumped up and ran away when I looked at them, there were people in trees, monsters stabbing babies and noises I can't really describe. I told Julius I needed to go to sleep. He stopped and looked at me. I told him I was scared and I couldn't go on and needed sleep. I cried a bit. OK, I cried quite a lot, pretty loudly, like a baby. He hugged me. He texted Lorna and arranged a meeting point where I could get in the car. I got in the passenger seat, was covered in blankets and passed out. It was 4.18 a.m.

When I woke up it was light, and I felt like shit. I could hear Lorna talking to Julius. I sat up and opened the door. It was 7 a.m. I had to move.

There was never any thought of not keeping going for me. My first thought was, You are going to be OK. You are doing your best. Get back to work. I got out of the car and was amazed that my legs worked – albeit slowly and sorely. After shitting in a Sainsbury's carrier bag in front of a number of troubled onlookers, I was back in the game. I was going to finish this.

The last seventeen miles were a painful joy. The weather was brilliant, the scenery was amazing. There were some super-unnecessary hills, some ridiculous mud and bogs, and everything hurt. But I could still run. I was amazed. Joe (my other pacer) and I ran/walked to our final crew stop, just seven miles from Worm's Head where I had coffee and doughnuts and then we were away – seven miles of sand, hills and clifftops all the way to the end. All the way to the finish of a dream. All the way to a reality I'd never really allowed myself to believe could happen.

Just before the end I stopped to throw up and do other unspeakable things to a public convenience and had a little cry. I didn't want to cry at the end. I wasn't sad. I was just incredibly proud and so, so relieved.

Julius, Lorraine and Lorna were waiting with Pickle just before the finish line, and we ran in together. Pickle hadn't got the memo – so seven-minute miles was the order of the day for her. I was overjoyed to see her. My baby. She dragged me to the gate and jumped all over me. I finished the Wild Horse 200 in eighty-one hours and eighteen minutes. I had come in first female.

So much shit went wrong on this run. I was told by many people to eat before I was hungry and sleep before I was tired. I didn't stick to either piece of advice. Early on I changed my plan based on a thought about something that was not true: People expect me to win, I will let them down if I don't. Nobody thought that. I thought that. Me. But the crucial thing is that I noticed I had moved the goalposts based on thought, and I chose to turn it around. I had the tools to do that.

Although I am of course thrilled with the outcome, it does not define the experience in any way. It's a nice added bonus. What defines this experience is that I managed to unfuck my mistakes and sort out the shitty committee part of my brain when I needed to, because I have worked tirelessly to be able to do that. That is more of a win than coming first will ever be.

I learnt more about myself in those eighty-one hours than I have in years of reading, coaching and therapy. I used this event to put all the stuff I have learnt into action. It was a case study. I am a coach; I talk to people about this stuff all day, every day, but to put it into action myself and to see it work was all-powerful. My recovery to this point is bang on. My feet, however, look like exotic dog treats. But they'll recover. We do recover.

THANKS

There aren't enough words to thank the people that hold me up and keep the foundations from wobbling. First thanks go to Kirsty Reade, my commissioning editor, friend and the reason you get to read these words. I met her up a mountain in the Lake District and that was that. She's one of the kindest, most compassionate, funny and clever women I know. Thank you and the Vertebrate team for everything; you made a bit of a dream come true here, mate. So, thank you from the bottom of my heart.

The forever support team: my mum for being unwavering in her love and care even when I was at my worst. I'm sorry if I scared you, Mum. My brothers, sister, nieces and nephews. I love you all deeply, but special thanks to Janey and Olly; without you both I just wouldn't be here. Thanks to Cat, Strick, Freya and Anshu for being there in the good times and putting up with me during the bad. I hope this goes some way to explaining things – and I am sorry for the times I hurt you. To KP – Katherine, I love the bones of you. Thank you for bringing Pickle into my life.

And to Pickle. Obviously. The one and only. You help me be the person I want to be every day. Great job, Pie.

Other huge high fives to Julius Naim – my best friend. Unflinching in your friendship and unconditional love, at times highly annoying, and proud dad to Pickle. Thank you for being the greatest friend. Lorna Spayne – constantly patient and kind throughout it all – I couldn't ask for a greater woman to have in my corner. Sarah Underwood – you know why. You were all there when others weren't, and I won't forget it. Love and respect always to my Arc/Spine/whatever crew – Ross, Joe, Lorraine, Lawrence (he's done the Spine, you know … doesn't like to talk about it) and Anna B for being the ultra-support dream team and making me laugh on WhatsApp. I promised I'd thank Damian Hall. I don't know why but I'll lump him in with this lot.

Hats off to David Miller for shooting the images that adorn the cover of this book and the ones you see all over my website – an incredible talent and a lovely man to boot. Thanks to Paul and Simon from the Biffy Clyro team for allowing me to use their lyrics and just being fucking great, and a massive kiss to Anna Harding for being Anna Harding. To every band featured on that playlist, thank you. You help people manage every day. That is a gift.

Thanks to the race directors and people that make the running stuff possible. Where would we be without you? Unsung heroes. Andy and Gemma at White Star Running, James Elson and everyone at Centurion Running, the Centurion ultrarunning team, Rhys Jenkins and all at Pegasus, Ferg and the MudCrew team, Paul Albon and the Big Bear team – there are hundreds of people I could mention here, but these guys are the ones most likely to give me free races. The architects of adventure, the people that create the stuff we love to do and support it – Gary T, Stu Smith, Joe Faulkner, David Scott, Nick and Hannah, Kate, Ross and all at RAW. Thank you for helping me up mountains, across deserts and through jungles. Thanks for helping me believe I could do it. To the Run Brit TP team – James, Jools, Jaques, Rachel, Amanda, Martyn, Joe, Ross and Lorna. What a fucking ride that was. I will never forget that time we spent together and never forget how you all inspired me to be a bit of a better human.

To everyone in the Ultra Awesome Facebook group for providing me with direction, purpose and constant inspiration. To my clients past and present – I am so grateful I get to do the job I do and I am humbled you trust me with your running lives. Make sure you do your S&C. No excuses.

Thank you to my sponsors at inov-8 – a brand that has supported and championed me and never asked me to be anything I'm not. Thanks to the National Running Show and especially Mike Seamen for all the opportunities and his belief in me right from the start.

There are a lot more supporting artists in this story – a lot – and not enough space to list them all here. I am lucky to have so many good people around me, and I don't have the time or word count to make this work fairly, so if I forgot to write your name here, I've left a little space for you to write it yourself.

Thanks to ________________ – without you I'd be nothing.

Finally, thanks to the entire ultrarunning community – all of you – just for existing. One Community. One Love. Blue were a fucking great band, weren't they?

FURTHER READING

For making me feel like I'm not the only one:
A Little Life – Hanya Yanagihara
A Million Little Pieces – James Frey
Man's Search for Meaning – Viktor E. Frankl
The Goldfinch – Donna Tartt
The Secret History – Donna Tartt
The Midnight Library – Matt Haig

For describing the music industry better than I could:
Kill Your Friends – John Niven
Bodies – Ian Winwood

For helping me get sober:
The Unexpected Joy of Being Sober – Catherine Gray
Sunshine Warm Sober – Catherine Gray
Glorious Rock Bottom – Bryony Gordon
We Are the Luckiest – Laura McKowen
The Sober Diaries – Clare Pooley

For helping me get my shit together:
The Happiness Trap – Russ Harris
Reasons to Stay Alive – Matt Haig
The Practice of Groundedness – Brad Stulberg
Do Hard Things – Steve Magness
Quit: the Power of Knowing When to Walk Away – Annie Duke
Peak Performance – Brad Stulberg and Steve Magness
Beyond Possible – Nimsdai Purja

For helping me to stay running when I wanted to fuck it all off:
Ultramarathon Man – Dean Karnazes
Running Man – Charlie Engle
Reborn on the Run – Catra Corbett

HELP/CRISIS LINES (UK ONLY)

In a life-threatening emergency, or if you believe you are a risk to yourself or others, always call 999.

HelpGuide
An incredible resource for you or someone you know who is in crisis; offers international options as well as UK-based services.
helpguide.org

DEPRESSION AND MENTAL HEALTH

The Samaritans
24-hour support on the phone or online.
116 123
www.samaritans.org

Mind
Helplines and crisis resources at your fingertips.
0300 123 3393
www.mind.org.uk

CALM
Campaign Against Living Miserably
Specialises in help for men but there to help everyone.
0800 58 58 58
www.thecalmzone.net

ALCOHOL AND ADDICTION

Recovery Runners
Leeds-specific group offering runs and informal chat every Sunday.
recoveryrunners21@gmail.com

Drinkline

If you are worried about how much you or someone you know is drinking, call them weekdays 9 a.m. to 8 p.m., weekends 11 a.m. to 4 p.m.
0300 123 1110

Alcoholics Anonymous

Hundreds of groups across the country offering help and support to individuals struggling with alcoholism.
0800 917 7650
www.alcoholics-anonymous.org.uk

Turning Point

Offering help and support across the country at a number of clinics.
www.turning-point.co.uk

Alcohol Change

Help and support for families and individuals.
alcoholchange.org.uk

ABOUT THE AUTHOR

Allie Bailey is an ultrarunner, coach, speaker and podcaster who has run in some of the most extreme places in the world. She was the first woman to run 100 miles across frozen Lake Khövsgöl in Mongolia and to run the full length of the Panama Canal. She has crossed the inhospitable Namib Desert three times, run the length of the Outer Hebrides and completed a 1,000-mile off-road version of the classic Land's End to John o'Groats route in just thirty days. Allie has finished over 200 marathons and ultramarathons all over the world, but the most remarkable thing about all of these achievements is that she accomplished most of them while battling depression and alcoholism. Although running ultimately became the vehicle that helped buy Allie the time to recover from a number of severe mental health breakdowns, it did not save her. In fact, there were times when it made her battle all the more difficult. After a seismic mental health crisis in 2021, Allie finally admitted to herself and those around her that she was an alcoholic and started her recovery. She left behind a dream career with major record labels and adventure companies and now works as a coach with a broad range of runners and endurance athletes, helping them unlock their full potential. In 2022, she was named as one of the most inspiring female adventurers in the UK by the *Guardian*, and she has appeared on numerous mainstream TV programmes including *The One Show* and *Lorraine*. She lives in Yorkshire with her rescue dog, Pickle.

www.alliebailey.co.uk

Made in United States
Orlando, FL
05 April 2024

45489212R00117